# REDEEMED
# BY GRACE

A Journey of Faith, Failure,
and Finding God's Purpose

James Dicks

Commerce Publishing
Lake Mary, Florida

Redeemed by Grace
© 2025 James Dicks

Published in the United States by Commerce Publishing
103 Commerce St, Suite 140
Lake Mary, Florida 32746

ISBN 979-8-9991072-0-6 (paperback)

This is a work of nonfiction. The events and experiences described are true to the best of the author's knowledge. Some names and identifying details have been changed to protect the privacy of individuals.

Unless otherwise noted, Scripture quotations are taken from the ESV® Bible (The Holy Bible, English Standard Version®), copyright © 2001 by Crossway, a publishing ministry of Good News Publishers. Used by permission. All rights reserved.

Printed in the United States of America

10 9 8 7 6 5 4 3 2 1

# DEDICATION

To my wife, Deb, my rock and constant support.

To my children, James and Jacki, you inspire me daily.

And to God, who never gave up on me

# ACKNOWLEDGEMENTS

To that end, in order as they may appear in this book, I will stick to first names unless they are family members:

Those early years: My mother, Marcia, has been my biggest fan and has shown me the unwavering love of a mother for her firstborn. I love you, Mom! My father had his challenges, and we had ours, but by the grace of God, in those final years we were able to have some of our best times. I have always admired his entrepreneurial spirit and creativity in structuring real estate deals. I miss him every day.

My grandfather JR, those fond memories of fishing and his warning that "Gators love Yankee meat." My grandmother June, a special relationship that can never be forgotten. She was someone who stepped in during times of need, and I was blessed to have her close during some of my biggest personal struggles. I will always miss her.

My immediate family: My sister, with whom I share a fantastic bond, only a year apart and close our entire lives. All those years of bickering, as my parents would say, only made us stronger. My nieces Jilly and Jaycee bring me such joy. My brother, Justin, with whom I've built a strong bond over the last five years; his wonderful wife, Amanda; and my two nephews, Levitt and Trip, whom I treasure watching play football and baseball.

Extended family: Aunt Joyce, my "grandmother in every way that mattered," who raised my mother and, at 93, is still going strong. Uncle Wyndall, who passed in 2019 and whom I miss every day, was like a grandfather to me. My stepmother Jewel stepped in where my father couldn't and made such a difference in my life, along with her husband Steve, who treats me like a son to this day.

Uncle John has been there as far back as I can remember, his commitment to helping me become a better man means everything. My Aunt Sharon has shown me love and kindness and has one of the biggest hearts I know.

Uncle Jack helped me grow and picked me up when I fell (which was often), teaching me important lessons in business and life that shaped who I am today. Aunt Linda supported my uncle whenever I needed help and was there for me consistently. Larry, my uncle's law partner, has been by my side through personal, professional, and legal challenges. Buddy, my uncle's business partner, provided inspiration during my early Christian journey and those formative years of learning about faith.

Faith mentors: Arthur Blessitt, the evangelist who carried a cross around the world and led me to Christ when I was 17. That moment changed everything. Dr. Joel Hunter, pastor at Northland Church, guided my early adult faith journey. Pastor Shaddy Soliman at Lake Mary Church, whose method of diving deep into Scripture has helped me grow tremendously.

Military and service family: Mike, my Marine friend, whose discipline and example inspired me to join the Corps, and his brother, Tom, a Catholic priest and Navy chaplain. All my brothers and sisters from ESGR who served alongside me for over a decade.

Business partners and mentors: Bob Reynolds, my dear friend and "personal realtor" who passed in 2017, a man of tremendous spiritual depth who helped shape my direction after the Marine Corps. Rocky, one of my first PremiereTrade employees who has been with us for 20 years, overseeing our technology.

Scott Prewitt, vice president of my development company, who I've worked with for over 35 years. Don Prewitt, Scott's father, whose vision created the sheriff's foundations and who calls me his son.

Community and neighbors: Kristy and Doug, whose monthly Bible study in our neighborhood has been instrumental in my renewed closeness with God. Kristy's mother, Mimi, can recite the Bible and draws me in every time I hear her speak the Word.

Special friends who shaped key chapters:

Tyler Benzel, like a brother, I miss our early morning Starbucks and Wall Street Journal conversations. I appreciate all that you've done and continue to do. I look forward to our next lunch.

Sergeant Major Brian Battaglia, I am honored to be your friend and Marine brother. Thank you for your leadership and unwavering service to all who have worn the uniform. Semper Fi.

Mike Schultz, my army battle buddy and true inspiration, someone I speak to regularly who has given his entire career to the Army.

Nick Nanton, you inspire me every day. I'm proud of everything you've accomplished and all you're doing. I'll ride shotgun on any journey you want to take, just say the word.

Duncan's memory stays with me every day. You were the ultimate fishing partner and road warrior. We had so many adventures, and your memory will always be with me. Rest in peace.

Charlie, you're a rock star in real estate, and I've learned a great deal from you. Your journey with sobriety inspired my own and changed my life forever.

Dave, after 45 years of friendship, I still wish you nothing but the best. Keep aiming for the stars, we've come a long way, and there's more ahead.

Jerry Smith, we've been through a lot together, starting back in the DNA Pulse days. We've tackled big challenges, and I know there's more ahead.

There are so many others I've met along the way, through baseball, business, or just crossing paths at the right time. You know who you are. I'm thankful for the part you've played in my story.

To all of you, thank you. This book wouldn't exist without the moments and memories we've shared.

And most of all, thank You, God. You never gave up on me. You put these people in my path, and I'm better for it.

# TABLE OF CONTENTS

# PREFACE

This This book has been in my heart for more than a decade. I've written business books, shared strategies, and built companies, but this is the first time I've taken the time to write about something more personal, my journey of faith. It's something I've wanted to do, but until recently, I hadn't felt I could do it. That has changed. Typically, when I write a book, I start with an idea, then the table of contents, and then write the chapters. This time was different. I was overwhelmed with the need to write my testimonial. I have always wanted to write my memoir to date, but every time I sat down to do that, I was unable to create the chapters and fill them in. This time was different. As you will read, my inspiration was faith inspired.

I did something I had always wanted to do and tried in the past, dictation. I sat down over a few days and dictated the rough draft of this book. It flowed in chronological order, opening up my long-forgotten memories.

Over the last couple of years, several things have aligned in my life that have pushed me to stop putting it off and finally start writing. One of those things was finding a home at Lake Mary Church, a place that has become central to my walk with God. The church recently celebrated its 15th anniversary, and I've witnessed how it has helped shape lives, including my own. Pastor Shaddy Solomon and the people there have reminded me what it looks like to live boldly in faith and be part of something greater than yourself.

Around the same time, we started a Bible study in our neighborhood. It was something simple, just friends and neighbors gathering to discuss Scripture and its application to everyday life. It was great getting to know neighbors I hadn't connected with before. The biggest thing for me was the personal testimonials, where people shared their vulnerabilities and their walk with Christ.

Another big moment for me was watching my wife, Deb, get baptized. My son and his wife were baptized shortly before Deb. Seeing her faith grow has meant so much to me. It reminded me that we all have our own journey with God, but He has a way of bringing them together. Watching her take that step moved me.

While writing this book, I began to feel that my testimonial is something that other people reading might be inspired to take their next step in their faith. That's who this book is for.

This book isn't a polished religious book. It's not perfect. It's full of real stories, some joyful, some painful. There have been times when I've struggled, times when I've gotten it wrong, and times when I've felt completely lost. I have always felt that God was there throughout it all. Writing this book, I can see just how true that is. I didn't always see it at the time, but I know He never left me.

As I wrote this, I thought a lot about grace. Not the kind you earn, but the kind that changes everything. I've had second chances and been lifted up when I probably didn't deserve it. And I've realized that God's grace has carried me further than I ever could have gone on my own.

I've also learned something else, something I wish I had known much earlier in life: God comes first. I didn't always put Him first. I didn't always live like I should. But with age comes wisdom, and now I see that keeping God first is the only way to truly walk in peace and purpose. This book stands as a constant reminder of that.

I am not saying this is easy to do and that we can do this all the time. That's why we have people in our lives that God puts in front of us at the right times, to reinforce that God comes first with their personal stories and testimonials. You can get that from friends and family, from church, from the Bible, and your neighbors.

I hope when you read this, you don't just hear my story, you see pieces of your own. Maybe you've wondered if God has forgotten you. Maybe you've questioned if it's too late to turn things around. It's not. You're not too far gone. If He can work through someone like me, He can work through you.

This book is part of my walk, not the end of it. I'm still learning. I'm still growing. And I'm still writing. These chapters reflect what God has done in my life, and I know there's more ahead. I'm just thankful for every step.

Thank you for reading. And thank you for letting me share what God has done and is still doing in my life.

Proverbs 16:3 says, "Commit to the Lord whatever you do, and He will establish your plans." That's exactly what I'm doing with this book, committing it to Him and trusting Him to use it however He sees fit.

# INTRODUCTION

## *A Daily Prayer and Purpose*

Heavenly Father, thank You for this day: for the breath in my lungs and the strength to face whatever lies ahead. I ask that You guide me, shape me, and help me make good decisions. Let my words be kind, my actions be just, and my heart be open to the lessons You place before me. Help me to walk in Your will and be a reflection of Your grace. May this book serve as a vessel, not just for my testimony but as a means of bringing hope to someone who may need it most.

This prayer is how I should begin every day, in prayer and reflection. I don't always start my day like this, though I do start with a prayer. Writing this book has taught me a great deal about my faith and has helped me refine my prayers. My relationship with God hasn't always been strong, but it has always been present. Sometimes quiet. Sometimes distant. But in recent years, it has become louder, clearer, and more central to my life. That's why this book exists.

This isn't just my story. It's a story of grace, mistakes, forgiveness, and redemption. I felt compelled, truly called, to write it. If even one person is helped, encouraged, or comforted by something within these pages, then all the effort, time, and vulnerability that went into writing this book were worth it.

I used to think my writing was too elementary. But what I've learned is that simplicity can be powerful. My voice may not be polished in the academic sense, but it's real. It's relatable. It's honest. And in that clarity and sincerity, I hope others find something true they can hold onto.

The words in this book come from a real place, sometimes broken, sometimes bold, but always seeking God's will. I'm not a pastor. I'm not a theologian. I'm a man who has stumbled, stood back up, and kept going with God at his side. I did not always remember that, but as I got older, I could see it.

Writing this book is something I've thought about for more than a decade. When I first set out to write, I figured I would quickly complete ten or fifteen chapters and be done with it. And I did, at least initially. But when I went back and reread what I had written, forgotten memories began to resurface. That's when I knew I had more to tell.

So, I returned to the draft, again and again, making sure I included the stories that mattered. Along the way, I also felt convicted to include Scripture, at the right moments, in the right places. I carefully selected verses that fit the themes and emotions in each chapter.

For those who want to reflect further, I've included all the Scripture references in an appendix at the end of the book. For me, it was a renewed awakening in my faith and cause of study and reflection as I chose the right verses. I would read through several chapters and then expand on the verse, studying more of the chapter. I have grown in my faith from writing the book.

Proverbs 3:6 says, "In all your ways acknowledge Him, and He will make your paths straight." That's exactly what I'm trying to do with this book, acknowledge Him in every story, every struggle, and every victory. May God use this book to bless those who need to hear these words.

# CHAPTER 1

# The Early Years

## *Foundation and Family - Seeds of Faith*

Let's start with my first experiences of church. My mother's sister took my mom in when she was only two years old and raised her. That's my Aunt Joyce, a great woman, and her husband, Uncle Wyndall, who passed away on October 28, 2019, and is missed every day. Though they were technically my aunt and uncle, they were my grandparents in every way that mattered.

After all, I was the first grandson, and to this day, my 93-year-old Aunt Joyce and I speak regularly. She watches every Rays baseball game, and she and I often talk baseball and have the greatest conversations. They were and are pillars in our family, and their involvement in church laid the early foundation of my Christian life.

When I was a baby and toddler, my sister Jana and I attended church with my mother and father. Something I didn't realize until recent conversations with my mother while preparing for this book. My father had mentioned numerous times to my mother about pursuing a career in politics or even becoming a minister. That was something new for me to hear, but I could see that. My other uncles are great speakers as well, and both sound like preachers in front of a room, my uncle John especially. My dad loved getting dressed up and attending church with us, along with Joyce and Wyndall, at the Brandon Baptist Church.

We spent Easters at my aunt and uncle's every year for as long as I can remember. Only after my uncle Wyndall passed away in 2019 did Easter slow down. The whole family on my mom's side would go for Easter. It was such a big thing, taking a family picture in front of the house, I have lots of them throughout the years.

One thing that stands out is that we would hunt Easter eggs in the yard every year. We would go to church, come home, have dinner, take photos, and hide eggs. Later, my wife and I would do the same for our kids, a full circle.

My first real church experience that I can remember was at First Baptist Church of Brandon, Florida. I would go on to have many Christmas Eve services there, and I even attended in my dress blues straight from Parris Island as a Private First Class in the United States Marine Corps. One of my last memories there was about six years ago for my uncle's funeral.

As children, we traveled from Vermont to Florida during the spring, which was mud season; essentially, no one wanted to live there at that time. I remember feeling, at a young age, like I didn't fit in, especially at church. My grandparents on my father's side were longtime members of the Plant City Baptist Church, and we attended there regularly as well. My awkward teenage years, struggling to connect, attending youth groups, my sister's first wedding, and my grandmother's funeral all happened there.

In those early years, it was my Aunt Joyce who ensured I was always taken care of. She and Uncle Wyndall were Sunday School teachers, and she eventually became a schoolteacher and the principal at the church's school before retiring. I attended traditional Sunday School and sat through numerous church services. I can't say I paid much attention back then, and I'm a bit embarrassed to admit that now, but I was young.

But I do have one of my earliest memories of personal prayer, which came from my mother. When I was around five, we moved into our first real home in Mount Snow, Vermont. Before that, for the first few years of my life, we lived in my father's hotel. My dad had taken six hotel rooms and combined them to create a small place for us to live. I was about three years old, watching my father cut the first hole between two rooms, one was mine, and the other was my sister's.

My sister and I used to crawl through that hole, and we thought it was the coolest thing until they were able to put a door in. We took three rooms and converted them into a kitchen and family room and then used one more room for my parents. Small, but it worked.

It was in that first real home in Mount Snow where my mom taught me my first prayer. Every night, she would tuck me in, and we'd say together: "Now I lay me down to sleep,

I pray the Lord my soul to keep. If I should die before I wake, I pray the Lord my soul to take. God bless Mommy, Daddy, and everyone in the whole world. Amen." I was so young, but I remember saying that prayer every single night. Looking back now, my mother was planting the first seeds of faith in my heart, teaching me that talking to God was as natural as breathing. Even at five years old, I was learning that God was someone I could turn to, someone who cared about me and my family.

Proverbs 22:6 says, "Start children off on the way they should go, and even when they are old, they will not turn from it." My mother was doing exactly that, setting me on a path of faith that would sustain me through all the challenges ahead.

My struggles fitting in started early. In kindergarten and first grade at Mount Snow, Vermont, it wasn't good, I felt like an outsider. My father owned a local well-known ski resort, and the other kids resented me for it. I can clearly remember some of the things that were traumatizing, things like being bullied at the bus stop, going back home before the bus came, not wanting to go to school, and feeling sick because of the verbal and physical attacks I knew would happen that day.

I still remember the name of one of the bullies that lived in my neighborhood. When at school, I was ridiculed and humiliated. PE was a particular area of abuse, making fun of me and my last name. I hated it; I hated school. Not to say

I didn't create some of my embarrassing moments. I don't know where I stood in my faith as a first grader, but there was one instance when I should have been praying.

It was a cold winter morning, with snow all around and blue skies; I can remember it as if it were yesterday. I am not making this up, it did happen. There I was, in front of the school, perhaps putting the flag up for the day, and the metal flagpole, glistening in the morning sunlight, looked inviting.

So yes, what did I do? I stuck my tongue on it, and of course, it froze to the pole. I was so embarrassed I immediately just ripped it off, and to this day, there is probably an outline of the skin I left on that pole 52 years ago. I should have said a prayer, for sure.

Another time when prayer would have been helpful was during my first- and second-grade school experience. You must keep in mind the school was K-12 at that time, and there were a few hundred kids. We took a field trip on the bus, about an hour's drive from the school to a small theme park called Santa's Land USA in Putney, Vermont, which opened in 1957. It was a small, Christmas-themed amusement park that featured Santa's workshop, elves, antique car rides, and a mini-golf course. It remained open for over 50 years before eventually closing.

Coming home on the bus, my mother was picking us up at school. The only problem was that my sister was not on the bus. She got left there, and my parents were frantic as we searched for her until we ultimately received a call from the park that they had found her. I felt very worried about her. In the end, all was good. My father went and picked her up.

Another early memory where prayer would have helped was when I was in second grade, and my mom sent me to summer camp in Brattleboro, Vermont, about an hour from home. I have very distinct memories of this, a small cabin with three walls and an open screen front, sitting on the mountainside.

If it weren't for my reluctance to be there and possibly being a little older, it would have been pretty neat; the mountains and views were spectacular. I remember the pool at the bottom of the hill, the lunchroom (more like a pavilion), and the arts and crafts.

I also remember being bullied by other campers and crying myself to sleep, praying that my mom would come get me. Yet another story from my early years has contributed to my faith's strength, resilience, and desire to help others. The horrible experiences of the school continued; when we returned to Florida for part of third grade after coming down from Vermont to avoid the spring mud season, I attended Wilson Elementary School in Plant City. I tried to forget that horrible experience, being bullied and ridiculed; not the first time I have used these words, and it won't be the last time in this book.

What I remember most was the teacher who, for whatever reason, didn't like me, and she made a point to call me out in front of the class when she could. A few times, I was sent to the principal's office, and my mom was called, most likely because I was acting out or had embarrassed myself and wanted to leave.

One particular instance was when the teacher asked us students to share in class what they had done over the winter break. When it was my turn, I shared about visiting Washington, D.C., the Capitol, and the White House, and all I remember is that she made me sit down and embarrassed me in front of the entire room.

My mom told me that the teacher said, "How do you think the other kids feel when he shares that?" The teacher felt I was entitled and should not be sharing with the others. It was a very unpleasant experience and one that I related to throughout the rest of my schooling.

1 Peter 5:10 says, "And the God of all grace, who called you to his eternal glory in Christ, after you have suffered a little while, will himself restore you and make you strong, firm and steadfast." Even then, in those moments of childhood pain and humiliation, God was preparing me for the strength that would come later. What felt like overwhelming suffering in those young years was God's way of building resilience and character that would serve me throughout my life.

When I was nine, my parents sent me to live with Aunt Joyce and Uncle Wyndall for the start of fourth grade in 1977. It was hard leaving my parents and sister behind in Vermont. They felt I needed to be in Florida and attend a private school to catch up academically.

I struggled to fit in and was bullied for a long time through school to about the start of 10th grade, a defining moment where I stood up for myself. My last name, "Dicks," didn't help, and being called "Jamie" by my family only made things worse. Coming from Vermont, the school system in Florida was a huge adjustment for me.

That turning point came in the face of personal hardship. My parents and sister moved back to Florida about three months after I did. I bounced around between my grandparents in Plant City and my aunt and uncle in Brandon during those three months, attending a private school in Valrico. Coming from schools in Vermont, this was a real eye-opener.

On Christmas Day that year, when I was nine and in fourth grade, my father walked out. What followed was a long, contentious divorce. My sister and I felt like pawns in a battle we didn't understand. We were poor, and my mother, young and trying her best, struggled. These were some of the hardest years of my childhood.

Making things worse, my mother was informed by the Plant City Baptist Church Bible group that she could no longer be in that group and had to join the singles group.

16

She shared with me how humiliating that was, and that was the catalyst for her to go to the Methodist Church, where a close family friend was the organist.

My mom told me that my uncle Wyndall was not very happy about that. Here, they are Southern Baptist and very proud of it. My mom said he called them "candle burners" and insisted that she bring my sister and me to Brandon Baptist Church on Sunday, about a 40-minute drive each way. So, we didn't go to the Methodist church for long, but it planted another small seed. The real turning point in my young Christian life was just around the corner, one that would have such a profound impact that it remains crystal clear 45 years later.

Due to my insecurities, lack of self-confidence, and low self-esteem, I began associating with friends who were probably not good for me. I embarked on a journey that, as you will discover in these pages, lasted for most of my young adult life. Usually, friends much older than me, I felt like I fit in better. Even in my neighborhood, I was bullied, didn't fit in, and didn't even want to be there. Those scars run deep, and even as a young kid, I can remember all the bully's names.

Those difficult years were tough, but I realize how fortunate I was to have had my grandmother, June, in my life. She became one of my greatest sources of stability during some of my most uncertain times. My grandmother was part of a legacy that went back generations in

Hillsborough County. Her parents, my great-grandparents, were pillars of the community.

My great-grandmother Gladys Simmons was someone I had a close relationship with as a young child. In the mid-80s, I would ride by on my bike and see her. I loved her and had a close relationship with her. As her family was getting busy, she used to enjoy my visits.

She always had a fresh, hand-made pound cake that I was more than happy to partake in. She had a passion for crochet, and in her house, there would be pillows and afghans by the pounds, and of course, that's what family got at Christmas time. Some of my earliest Christmases were at her home.

I was unable to meet my great-grandfather, as he passed away before I was born, but he was a staple in Hillsborough County. He was a farmer with roots dating back to the late 1800s in the area, but his passion lay in politics. My Great-grandfather served on the county commission for 28 years, including 18 years as chairman of the board. There are parks and schools named after my great-grandparents.

My grandmother June carried on that legacy of caring for her family. I was essentially homeless with no clear direction in my life, bouncing around in the early 90s, and I ended up living with her on a few occasions. She would greet me with open arms every time, and I think she loved having me there.

We would have some great conversations. I would help out around the house, and we would talk about God and her past experiences. I was always asking about my great-grandparents and our family history.

Some of the lowest times in my life were at her house. I would pray in my room at night, emotionally and desperately trying to find solutions to my situations, personally and financially, questioning life and not wanting to go on. It was a very difficult time, and my grandmother, June, helped me through it. In those dark moments, when I felt like I had nowhere else to turn, I would talk to God like He was right there in that room with me, because He was.

But I also remember the other side of that. My grandmother was getting dementia and early-onset Alzheimer's. I would see that take control of her through the years I lived with her, and it got worse every day, week, month, to the point that she was no longer able to live in her home. When I moved to Orlando, I lost those very missed days of being able to spend time with her.

When I got back from the Marine Corps, I had to visit her in a nursing home, and after my son was born, my wife and I went to see her in a locked memory care facility. I remember praying for my grandmother and selfishly for me to be able to have compassion and make her feel as best as I could, even though she did not recognize me.

Alzheimer's is my biggest personal fear. My grandmother passed away from it after more than a 10-year battle. Today, my Uncle Jack, who has been such an important figure in my life and business, is now suffering from the same disease and has regressed substantially, adding even more urgency to my concerns and prayers that researchers can develop ways for people suffering from this horrible disease to live a better life. Alzheimer's is something I am passionate about, and I try to support any local efforts that contribute to that cause.

One of the most eye-opening jobs I ever had was working in supplies at Tampa General Hospital when I was probably 17 years old. Seeing what goes on behind the scenes in a hospital at such a young age gave me a perspective that most people don't gain until much later in life, if at all. First and foremost, God is there in the midst of pain, tragedy, heartache, and loss. God is still there. I have seen miracles firsthand there.

Tampa General was built around the old hospital, which was constructed in 1905, and the municipal hospital, which was built in 1927, forming the Tampa General Hospital site on Davis Island. My job in supplies was to deliver whatever was needed to all departments in the hospital, including the burn ICU, prenatal ICU, cardiac ICU, psych ward, pediatric ICU, and everything in between. I wore scrubs and traversed the hospital every day.

There was one particular delivery that always made me say a prayer before I started. To get to pediatrics, you had to travel through the old hospital from the new hospital, and the fastest way there was straight across. You would cut through on a middle floor, and as you rolled your cart through those halls, this was an abandoned section that had been empty for a long time, some lights were on, some off, some flickering. Some curtains were open, some closed, shadows everywhere.

You'd push your cart down this long, dimly lit hallway with hospital room doors open, half-open, or closed, and you would hear the clanging echoing down the corridor. As I started down that hallway, the clanging grew louder and louder because I was sprinting at full speed to the other side. This hospital scene was straight out of a Halloween movie. Finally, I would arrive on the other side where all was well, a joyful relocation to a place that humbled me.

Coming home from work, I used to think that all Americans should have to work at a hospital when they are younger, even if just as a candy striper volunteer. It will give you a perspective on life you will never forget. Working at Tampa General Hospital taught me an important lesson. When you see people fighting for their lives every day, when you watch families dealing with serious diagnoses, when you're around the reality of life and death, it changes how you look at your problems. The challenges I was facing didn't seem so big anymore.

That experience gave me a perspective that has stayed with me my whole life. I learned never to give up, to not feel sorry for myself for very long, and to always focus on finding solutions instead of just thinking about the problems. When you've seen what real struggle looks like, when you've watched people face the hardest moments of their lives with courage, you realize you can handle more than you think you can.

It's one of those jobs that teaches you about what matters and what doesn't. Those lessons have served me well through every challenge I've faced since then. Working at Tampa General Hospital showed me that everyone faces struggles and challenges, and everyone needs compassion. It also showed me that most people are stronger than they realize and that difficult circumstances don't have to define you. You can face hardship with dignity, find ways to survive and overcome, and maintain hope even in dark times.

Isaiah 43:2 says, "When you pass through the waters, I will be with you; and when you pass through the rivers, they will not sweep over you. When you walk through the fire, you will not be burned; the flames will not set you ablaze." Even in that hospital setting, surrounded by pain and suffering, I was learning that God's presence helps us through our darkest moments.

There was a local friend named Allan whose story became a sobering reminder of how different paths can lead to tragedy. We hung out constantly and got into typical trouble, like the time we caught a three-foot alligator and somehow convinced ourselves to put it in his family's pool. His mother was not amused.

But Allan's story took a dark turn. His parents were well-off, and he had his own house at a young age, which became a gathering place for parties, drinking, and trouble. I lost track of him after junior high, but years later, I'd run into him occasionally. Each encounter was worse; he'd been in and out of jail and had even served a few years in prison. He'd become increasingly angry and confrontational with me about "leaving him behind" when I moved on with my life.

I found myself praying for Allan but also praying I wouldn't run into him. That prayer was answered in the most tragic way possible. Just before I was to be married, my mother called with devastating news: Allan had killed himself playing Russian roulette in front of a table of teenagers at one of his parties. He was 29 years old.

I remember the sinking feeling, wondering if there was something I could have done, something I should have done. I prayed for Allan, for his family, and especially for those young people who witnessed such a horrific event. I can't say I remember ever praying back then, but I do have flashbacks of how painful and uncertain that time was. I now know that God was planting seeds in me during those moments, setting the stage for the day when I would come to truly know Him.

Ecclesiastes 3:1 says, "To everything, there is a season and a time to every purpose under the heaven." Looking back on those early years, there was a time for struggle, a time for confusion, and a time for pain, but God was using each period to prepare me for what was ahead. Even though I didn't know it at the time, God was with me. God was working in my life, even when I couldn't see it. He was preparing me for what was coming next, including a relationship that would change everything.

In Chapter 2, I'll tell you about when I truly found Jesus, when I accepted Him as my Lord and Savior. But it was all those early years, with all the uncertainty and struggle, that got me ready for that moment. I've learned that God uses the hard times in our lives to prepare us for what He has planned.

# CHAPTER 2

# Finding Jesus

*The Moment That Changed Everything*

Everything changed when I was seventeen. The year was 1985, and I was a junior in high school, still dealing with all the emotional turmoil from my early years. The bullying, my parent's divorce, and feeling like I didn't fit in, especially with those in my class. I had no idea God was preparing me for what was to come. Back then, I was just trying to find to find my place.

My sister, a year younger than me, was singing in the choir at the Plant City Baptist Church. She was popular and involved, and all her friends were there. She spent a lot of time at that church, and through her, I became friends with some of the kids who went there.

These kids were different from the crowd I had been running with. They were in the church music department, where they played in the band, sang, and were really good Christians. For the first time in my life, I remember feeling like I belonged somewhere.

Feeling like I belonged was something I didn't have at school. Quite frankly, looking back, my sister was probably more suited to high school life. She was a cheerleader; she was more involved with the in-crowd. I certainly was not.

I tried, I tried to play football in my first year, 10th grade, at our high school. I played for the season on junior varsity, but that didn't do anything for me. I didn't make connections and didn't feel any better about myself. As I started to move through high school, I found myself hanging out more and more with a rougher crowd or an older crowd.

They were good people to me, and some of them I'm still close friends with after all these years. That rougher crowd became good friends, and no doubt some of them went on to do great things and have families to be proud of. Some, not so much. We were probably doing things we shouldn't have been doing, and I certainly wasn't acting as a good Christian would, though I didn't know any different at the time.

Things were still tough at home. We were struggling financially, and my parents were still going through their divorce after all those years. I remember it always seemed to be about money. We never really had any, and it made everything more difficult.

But I have to give my mom credit - she was working multiple jobs to keep us afloat. She was riding her bike to the community college to earn her associate's degree. She was then accepted at the University of Tampa, where she graduated in 1986.

But at the church, something felt different. I felt accepted. The more I hung out with the church kids, the more something felt different. For once in my life, I actually felt like I belonged somewhere that I fit in, something I needed in my life at that time.

That's when the youth convention was announced; it would change my life forever and put me on a different path, the one God wanted me to walk, not that I knew it at that time. One of the guys from our church was in his mid-twenties, which seemed older to us at the time, and he was part of a Christian contemporary group from Atlanta. It had been a huge recruiting process for him to get in, a serious audition period, and we were all excited for him. They were playing at the Curtis Hixon Hall in Tampa, which was a major convention center.

I remember that we all went to Tampa together, and this was a huge event. Thousands of people were there, and many fellowship groups from Baptist churches throughout the area attended. Again, I just felt like I belonged. I felt good being part of something bigger than myself, and I was with my sister.

The atmosphere was electric. The music was incredible, we got to hear our friend from Plant City play with this amazing Christian group, and the worship was unlike anything I had ever experienced. But it was the keynote speaker who captured my attention.

The speaker was Arthur Blessitt, and he was extraordinary. Arthur Blessitt was a man who had carried a twelve-foot wooden cross around the world, through every nation on earth. He had walked over 43,000 miles across six continents, sharing God's message.

He had been arrested countless times, faced persecution, and endured incredible hardships, all for the sake of spreading God's love. When he spoke, I felt he was speaking directly to me, and he has lived a life of faith, as evidenced by his journey. He wasn't just talking about Jesus; he had lived a life completely devoted to Him.

This man talked about his journey, about the people he had met, the miracles he had witnessed, and the transforming power of Christ. This speech wasn't some typical preacher talking about Jesus like He was just another guy from history class. He was talking about Jesus like He was sitting right there in the room like He actually cared about messed-up kids like me. When he told stories about the crazy things he'd seen God do all over the world, I was glued to every word.

But what got me wasn't the stories, it was him. You could just see it. This guy wasn't putting on a show. When he said that no one was too far gone for God, that no life was too broken for God to fix, I believed him because you could tell he'd seen it happen. I knew he meant it. He was probably living proof of it himself. You could see how much he loved Jesus.

Then came the moment that changed everything. Arthur asked if there was anyone in that massive auditorium who was ready to accept Jesus into their life, anyone willing to stand up and accept Jesus as their Lord and Savior. My heart was pounding. I felt something stirring deep inside me that I had never felt before. And I stood up.

Romans 10:9 says, "If you declare with your mouth, 'Jesus is Lord,' and believe in your heart that God raised him from the dead, you will be saved." That night, I got it. I really got it. I wasn't just saying the right words because that's what you do at church. This decision was real. This was me making a choice that was going to turn my whole life around.

To this day, I can still feel that moment. It's hard to explain; everything just made sense for the first time. All pain from being bullied, ridiculed, and low self-esteem was gone - maybe it was still there, but different somehow. Like I could take on anything now. I felt what many describe as a huge weight lifted off my shoulders. All of the problems that I'd had, all the family issues, all the bullying, all the years of not fitting in, it was like all this weight just lifted off my shoulders.

I think I even cried. I can remember my sister crying as well. Where I would normally have been socially awkward, I was consumed by the moment. I was surrounded by our group of friends and thousands of Christians, and I just soaked it all in. The presence of God was so real, so tangible in that moment. I felt loved in a way I had never experienced before, completely accepted, completely forgiven, completely new.

2 Corinthians 5:17 became real to me that night: "Therefore, if anyone is in Christ, the new creation has come: The old has gone, the new is here!" I felt like a completely new person walking out of that convention center.

But as we'll discuss in future chapters, accepting Jesus was just the beginning of my journey. The Christian life isn't about one moment of decision, it's about a lifetime of walking with Him, learning to trust Him, and growing in faith.

It wasn't too many months, maybe a year at most, after that time when I accepted Jesus that I fell away from the church. I continued hanging out with the same crowd I had been running with before. My church friends were good to me, but they just weren't the right crowd for a new Christian trying to grow in his faith. I got pulled back into things that I shouldn't have been doing, and I certainly wasn't living a good Christian life. I wasn't going to church regularly, and I wasn't able to apply all the things I had learned that night in Tampa.

But here's the thing, I knew that I had accepted Jesus. I knew that God was in my life, even when I wasn't living like it. And it was during the struggles that followed, when things became really difficult, that I would start to pray. Nobody taught me how to pray. Nobody showed me the "right" way to do it. I just prayed. I asked for help. I talked to God like He was right there with me, because He was.

There were many times during those years of finishing high school that were just very depressing, very low. There were moments when I felt like maybe I couldn't go any further, maybe I didn't want to. But it was God who was right there in my heart, Jesus, telling me that I could make it through. I'd wake up the next morning and somehow find the strength to do what I needed to do for that day.

Those were some really dark, rough times, and I attribute my ability to survive them to that one moment when I asked God to come into my life. Even when I wasn't living perfectly, even when I made mistakes and poor choices, that foundation was still there. The seed that had been planted in my heart that night in Tampa was still there, waiting to grow.

Jeremiah 29:11 reminds us, "For I know the plans I have for you," declares the Lord, "plans to prosper you and not to harm you, to give you hope and a future." Even in my darkest moments as a teenager, God had a plan for me. He was working even when I couldn't see it, even when I wasn't listening to Him.

The truth is, finding Jesus isn't just about a moment in time, it's about a relationship that grows and develops over the years. That night in 1985 was when I first said yes to Jesus, but it wasn't the last time I would need to surrender my life to Him. In the chapters that follow, we'll discuss how I've implemented my faith throughout the years, how I've learned from my mistakes, and how God has remained faithful even when I've not been faithful to Him.

But it all started with that moment of standing up in a convention center in Tampa, Florida, and accepting Christ our Lord and Savior. That's when my real story began, not the story of a perfect Christian, but the story of a broken young man who found hope, purpose, and unconditional love through Jesus.

And that changes everything.

# CHAPTER 3

# Wilderness Years

## *When Faith Goes Underground*

Graduating from high school in 1986 should have felt like freedom, but instead, it felt like stepping into quicksand. That moment of clarity I'd experienced at the Tampa convention seemed like a distant memory. The faith that had once felt so real was now buried somewhere deep inside me, surfacing only when I was desperate enough to pray.

The truth is, I got further away from God during those years. I continued to run in circles that weren't conducive to a productive lifestyle, and I started drinking more. The crowd I was hanging with were good people to me during some of my most challenging times, but some of them had lost their way as well. Looking back now, I can see how perilous that path had become.

I remember my sister telling me a story that shook me. She was singing in the choir at a Florida prison, Raiford in Starke, where death row is located. It was around the holidays when an inmate approached her and asked if she was James Dicks's sister.

She was startled, probably mortified someone at church might find out, but it turned out to be someone I knew. Someone I had probably partied with. He was in for murder.

That hit me hard. I realized I had known several people who ended up in prison for murder or manslaughter. These were people who had once been good to me. That scared me. I knew I could have easily been on the same path.

But even in those dark times, God was working in ways I couldn't see. Back in 9th grade, around 1983, I was struggling with something I didn't understand yet. I was having tremendous difficulty in school, especially with reading. The words would seem to move around on the page, and I'd get terrible headaches trying to focus.

I remember sitting in high school classes when everybody had to read a section of the lesson out loud. I would count the people in front of me and try to figure out where I would start reading. I was terrified at the thought of being embarrassed by my reading skills. I would try to read that section ahead of time so that I wouldn't fumble. The fear of humiliation was constant.

One of the most fascinating things while writing this book is the ability to look back at my journey with Christ. As we discussed earlier in the book, I was overwhelmed with the feeling that I needed to write this book. I was able to dictate it in a few short days, and as I was doing so, everything seemed to flow in chronological order, something that had previously prevented me from writing this before. I just couldn't get it all out, but that changed after attending a church service recently.

Once I finally got everything on paper and started working through the manuscript, I realized that my memories seemed to expand. The lost ones seemed to be found and clear, and I was able to add many of my life experiences to what I had already dictated. Furthermore, as the book in my mind was always intended to be my memoir, a way to remember, which is also the reason I wrote all the other books, what changed was my deep-seated feeling that God wanted me to write this. I was able to combine it with my walk with Christ, my spiritual journey.

As I wrote the book, I began to remember things associated with my faith, times I had prayed, times I needed to pray, divine intervention in my life, and God providing when he felt I needed it. After all, I am on his plan, not mine. That's exactly what happened with my dyslexia.

One night, I was out with a friend, and on the way home, I put on his amber-lens Ray-Bans. Suddenly, it was an eye-opener: literally. Everything became crystal clear, almost magnified. I asked if they were prescription, and he looked at me as if I were crazy. That's when I realized that color can affect how people with dyslexia see text.

I started wearing those glasses all the time, and I read better than ever before. Later, I found out my younger cousins had similar struggles, and their success with colored lenses led me to the Irlen Method. It was transformational. Around the age of 20, I was on a plane, and, for the first time, I completed reading a book cover to cover, "Clear and

Present Danger" by Tom Clancy, which was over 700 pages long. I was so proud of myself. Just writing this, I say thank You, God, for that experience and the solution: God's plan and his grace when you need it most.

What I thought was my biggest weakness turned out to be a hidden strength. Because I read slowly and had to concentrate on every word, I ended up comprehending almost everything I read. I even developed what seemed like a photographic memory, especially with numbers. Looking back now, I can see this was God preparing me for the business world I'd enter later.

Romans 8:28 says, "And we know that in all things God works for the good of those who love him, who have been called according to his purpose." Even when I wasn't walking closely with Him, God was there every step of the way.

Life was hard, and I was struggling. My last few years of high school were challenging, to say the least. I had finally gotten over most of the ridicule and bullying, but that was primarily because my friends were several years older than me, most of them had graduated already. And the others, no one would look at the wrong way.

Things at home, however, were not so good. My mom has always tried to make sure my sister and I had a place to go and a good home. Things didn't always work out, but not from her lack of trying. My mom, who had me at just eighteen, was doing her best. She graduated from the

University of Tampa in 1986, the same year I finished high school. She remarried, but my relationship with my stepfather was very difficult.

There were nights I'd sit in my room praying, hearing things no child should hear. My sister moved out even younger than me. She lived with a wonderful family that became like a second family to both of us. She graduated high school while living with them and is still close to them today, a testament to her faith.

After graduation in 1986, I took a year to work at my dad's ski resort in Vermont starting that October. He wasn't around much, as he was managing the hotel in Crystal River. I worked out, skied, stayed active, but the crowd up there wasn't on any Christian path. If anything, I was worse off there than in Florida.

My relationship with my father was nearly nonexistent. I would go to Crystal River to see him, but he would be busy. There were some summers in there as well, but we didn't get along very well. My sister didn't want to visit either. Those weekends often felt forced.

I had lots of jobs starting my junior year of high school. The first job I ever had was while in high school in DECA, a schoolwork program where I would leave school at 11 AM and go to work. My job was in Tampa, working for Ferman Oldsmobile. Steve, whom I write about later in the book, helped me get my first job because he was a partner with Mr. Ferman. Steve, many years later, became instrumental in my life, God's will and grace. Never knowing that God had a plan when I took that job.

Many other small jobs, a few worse than others. Working at the Tampa wholesale tree nursery was one to forget. I can remember the sights, smells, and experience to this day. I would get to work at 6:30 AM and start making sure the pots were in the rows straight, not hard to do until the sun starts to break the horizon over hundreds of acres of pots in rows. It's never-ending.

I distinctly remember one day standing at a section of plastic laid out for new rows of plants in pots. A tractor pulled up with about five trailers of potted plants, ready for me to offload. I quickly made short work of that, and then another tractor pulling many more trailers pulled up. I can remember saying, "Okay, got this," and I knocked those out. Then, yes, another tractor with more trailers pulled up. This rinse and repeat of the trailers continued until lunch. I was worn out and wondering if it would ever stop.

During lunch, I walked around to the back of one of the big warehouses, and there it was, the never-ending line of trailers on an automated system, an assembly line coming out with potted plants ready for a tractor to pick up. Workers inside the warehouse were planting the trees in pots and putting them on the assembly line of trailers. It would never stop. That's when I realized I might need to find a different job.

One of my big dream jobs, by the way, when you are fresh out of high school, your dream job is not so glamorous when you look back. I had many friends who went to work for Publix warehouse, the local grocery chain that started in Lakeland, Florida, and has gone on to be one of the largest chains in the southeast. So, I was never able to get a job at Publix. I tried many times, it just wasn't part of the plan that God had for me, the experiences that God wanted me to have.

So, I decided, 'Okay, I'll get a job at the Winn-Dixie warehouse.' There can't be much difference. I set out to get this job, and it took four months, going through multiple polygraph tests, written tests, and written exams, but I did get the job. It was the graveyard shift, and it was about 40 minutes from my house. I remember this like it was yesterday. I was so excited for my first night on the job.

I got there, and they wasted no time putting me to hard work. I walked into the warehouse, and the first thing I noticed was it was 41 degrees, and I was in short sleeves. Problem 1, but okay, I could handle that. Problem 2: I immediately noticed that I could not see the end of the warehouse. This thing stretched for a mile, kid you not, as far as you could see, it felt.

The inside of the warehouse was like an international airport, tugs, forklifts, trailers everywhere, very organized and clean. My job, easy. I would have a line of trailers come up to an assigned semi-trailer. I then transferred the produce and groceries from the trailer to the semi. Oh great, more trailers, and just like the tree nursery, they never stopped coming. It was a hundred trailers, it seemed, to fill a semi-truck. To this day, I have no idea how the poor truck driver unloaded what I had loaded for him.

I finished the first one an hour or so later and remembered I was no longer cold. That's when the manager came over and said, "Good job." I felt pride, not something I had often experienced at this age yet, and that's when the manager hit me right between the eyes with, "You can knock out one more before dinner." Lunch, whatever it would be, at midnight.

I looked down at the warehouse that I couldn't see the end of, and there must have been hundreds of semis backed in and ready to be loaded. That's when I realized I would not be retiring from that job. At my lunch break, or dinner, whatever, at midnight, I left and never looked back. Surely, God had more in store for me, and he certainly did.

That's about the time I headed to Vermont. I had always wanted to take some time and work at my dad's ski resort during the fall and winter when I got older. Now was the time. When I returned to Florida in the summer of 1987, I began working with my Uncle John. That is where my financial education and speaking experience started.

In 1987, I started working what I called "road crew" with my Uncle John. I would travel with him to his presentations, working the back of the room, answering questions, and doing administrative work. It was one of the few ways I could earn a decent income, although I was still living paycheck to paycheck and struggling financially.

In 1988, I began working more in the office of my Uncle Jack's business in Longwood, Florida. My Uncle John and Uncle Jack were doing similar stuff within the same industry and for some of the same companies.

Working with my Uncle Jack began what would become a crucial spiritual lifeline. My uncle's partner, Buddy, had attended seminary and was a strong Christian. On Wednesdays, we'd sit down after lunch and have Bible study together. Buddy taught me from the Bible and helped me understand how Scripture applied to real life. He knew I was struggling, and those sessions planted seeds that would grow later.

During this period, from 1987 to 1989, I also enrolled in a community college and attended sporadically for two years. I tried college, but it just wasn't for me. I was too involved in going out, drinking, and just not doing good things. What made it even harder was that dyslexia remained a real struggle, even with the colored lenses helping. Discussing learning disabilities today is much easier than it was in the past.

During this time, I would hit the road and do some events with my Uncle John. I recall a particular time during this period, one of those trips was to Atlanta, and I believe we were staying in the Buckhead area. I was running late to the airport, and I needed to make this flight on time. I had maybe $5 to my name; I was counting change just to get by. I knew that if I could get there on time, I could borrow maybe $40 from my uncle to get through the week until I got my paycheck. Missing this trip wasn't an option.

I arrived at the airport and missed my flight. I had to be there for a presentation that afternoon or evening, so there was nothing else I could do, I had to work it out. I got on another flight, and I remember praying specifically: "God, help me. I need to get to where I'm going. My job was on the line. I don't want to lose it. I need to be good at my job, and I don't know how I'm going to do this."

So, I just put one foot in front of the other, never giving up, and was able to catch the later flight to Atlanta. But because I missed my original flight, I also missed connecting with the group. Usually, when we traveled, there were several of us, and we'd have rental cars available to get us to our location. But everybody was already busy getting ready for the show that evening.

So, I got to Atlanta with my bags, and I had a couple of dollars to take MARTA, Atlanta's subway system. I was able to take that to the stop downtown, where I could catch a bus. I only had about $3 left, which was just enough to get me to about a mile and a half to two miles from the hotel where we were staying.

I got on the bus, and it dropped me off about two miles away from the hotel. I didn't want to call anyone for help. I certainly didn't want to call my uncle and ask for help. I just had to get to where I needed to be on my own.

I remember I had my luggage with me, and I had to carry it the entire two miles in Atlanta in June. It was sweltering hot, and I was sweating profusely, but I finally made it to the hotel. It's a lot better than walking to school in a snowstorm barefoot up a hill both ways, as my Uncle Wyndall would say.

God got me there. It cost me about $5 to do the whole thing. I was resilient enough to make it happen, and that's an important lesson I've carried with me ever since: if you don't give up, you can achieve your goals. However, if you give up, you'll never reach your goal.

Looking back, I can see that even in those desperate moments when I was counting change and praying for help just to get to work, God was building something in me. He was teaching me persistence, resourcefulness, and dependence on Him. Those weren't just struggles, they were preparation for everything that would come later.

In 1991, I was still working with my Uncle Jack and Buddy. I took my education to the next level, and I became a stockbroker. Like all the other brokers in the office, you could make more money as a broker than cold calling and setting up appointments. I was a broker until the mid-2000s, not necessarily an active one, though.

To stop my daily commute from Plant City to Longwood, I moved to Orlando with the help of my Uncle Jack, who had always looked out for me and given me many opportunities. However, around the end of 1991, my Bible studies with Buddy came to an end due to life circumstances changing.

Even with that spiritual foundation from those years of Bible study, I was still facing challenges in many areas.

When I moved to Orlando, I rented apartments I couldn't afford and lived above my means. I was broke, directionless, and too proud to ask for help. Around 1991, I experienced my first time being homeless, only a few days, I slept in my car and then couch surfing with a few friends. I was homeless more than once. Living in my car. It was terrifying, finding a place to park and sleep, hoping no one would knock on the window.

Something that you find yourself praying to God why, but more why you made such terrible decisions to have you end up there to begin with. I didn't have to be homeless, but I was too proud to ask for help. I can imagine that is similar to many who find themselves on the streets with no place to live.

As you grow in your relationship with God and your faith gets stronger, you don't ask the same questions; you realize that there is a reason if you don't know what it is. However, it makes you hyper-vigilant within your surroundings as if soaking it all in; there is something within this experience that matters, and you need to be aware. That sentiment is far more powerful today as I write this than it was going through my early years.

Those homeless experience were setting me up for the realization that I needed later in life when I would find myself in tough personal and financial situations. I had a choice, be homeless or ask for help, and my few experiences of being homeless ensured I would ask for help the next time, and that is what I did.

Many people find themselves in financial distress. All of them feel like mountains you can't climb or overcome, and some people feel so overwhelmed they can't go on, and that is the tragedy of financial depression. I have known a few in my life who ended their lives because of financial despair. It always shook me to the core because I have been there on more than one occasion, and a younger me has had those thoughts. However, God had a plan for me, and I learned to get up and do something, even if I didn't know what it was.

I can remember on more than one occasion; I had a car repossessed. That's a catalyst to make your financial despair worse. You are looking over your shoulder wherever you go, waiting for someone to take your car, and then what? There was no way to get around, no way to get anything done, and nowhere to live if you needed a place. That's a tough place to be and a tough feeling to have, especially when compounded by all the other financial problems that come with it. I watched the tow truck take my Jeep from outside my apartment.

I'd count change for gas. I went to a convenience store with fifty cents, trying to buy a box of macaroni and cheese for dinner. But I kept going. I didn't quit. And I prayed. Not in some perfect way, but the only way I knew how. I talked to God like He was right there, because He was.

During this difficult period, I recognized I needed help with my drinking. As I sit here writing this story, I was watching a movie about a man who lost his faith and turned to the bottle. He had a traumatic loss in his life, and he fell to the bottle, which estranged him from his daughter. In the end, he walked through the doors of the local church AA group and decided, with God's grace, to take a stand against his alcoholism. That brought vulnerability, and hard decisions brought back vivid memories of those days.

I wasn't someone who drank every minute of every day, but on weekends, I started sometimes at 8 AM, and I drank almost seven days a week from dusk to dawn. Watching this movie was very hard, to quit drinking is just hard to fathom, especially when you're caught up in that world.

I can remember my buddy Charlie from Tampa, who wasn't drinking. In 1992, Charlie took me to AA, my first experience with Alcoholics Anonymous. It was sobering, to say the least, pun intended.

I did not stand up and introduce myself, nor did I admit that I was an alcoholic, but what I got from that first meeting was that I was not alone. Many people, like myself, were there, trying to change and take control of their lives again, each with a different story.

The program and its roots in faith, God and the Bible, were a blessing. It reminded me of what I needed to do: I needed to get closer to God. I managed to quit drinking for a few months that year but eventually started again.

By the end of 1992, I made another attempt to quit drinking. Charlie in Tampa offered me a new opportunity, and I packed up my car and moved to Minneapolis to open a furniture store. I was determined to make a fresh start, and I found a local AA group there.

I met a man who was the manager of the storage units where I kept my furniture inventory. He was a recovering alcoholic for over 40 years and served as a sponsor to many people trying to get sober. I attended meetings there, and though I cannot remember if I ever stood up and said I was an alcoholic, what sticks with me all those years later was that I received my first 30-day coin, what they call a "chip" in AA. Although I had quit drinking before for longer periods, this was the first time it was officially recognized.

Unfortunately, being alone and struggling with the business challenges in Minneapolis, I started drinking again. This relapse was later in 1992. But that experience in AA, both in Tampa and Minneapolis, planted important seeds about recovery and the role faith plays in overcoming addiction.

I do remember the night I fell off the wagon while in Minnesota. I was out at a big country bar in Eagan, Minnesota. I felt awkward and self-conscious sitting by myself. That was all it took. I said I would have a few drinks, maybe three, but I recall that I was so drunk and didn't know why. It turns out that beer in Minnesota has twice the alcohol content as beer in Florida. Needless to say, I should have never driven home. I was disappointed with myself.

Was this God's plan for me? You have to look back and think, but it was, and I am writing this book because of that and many other paths I have taken with God's guidance.

Drinking and driving is a terrible thing and one that affects me personally every time I hear a tragedy or story of someone driving under the influence. I recently watched a movie that ended with the main character driving drunk, killing a pedestrian, and ultimately killing himself. That scenario was exactly what I was afraid of, and more so, harming innocent bystanders. That fear would later drive my final decision to quit drinking for good.

Psalm 34:18 says, "The Lord is close to the brokenhearted and saves those who are crushed in spirit." Even when I felt utterly alone, that foundation from Tampa was still there. Buried, but not dead.

It was during these wilderness years that I learned something important about faith. It doesn't always look like Sunday church or daily Bible reading. Sometimes, faith is a whisper in the front seat of your car when you don't know where to sleep. Sometimes, it's asking God for strength to make it through just one more day.

1 Peter 5:7 says to cast "all your anxiety on him because he cares for you." I was doing that without even realizing it was what a Christian should be doing.

In August 1994, I moved to Oklahoma City for another furniture business opportunity, and this time I quit drinking again. This period of sobriety would last until I graduated from Marine Corps boot camp later that year. But that transition and what came next became a turning point and foundation for who I would become.

But that's a story for the next chapter. For now, what matters is this: God was working, even in the wilderness, even when I couldn't see it, even when I wasn't cooperating. Sometimes, the deepest growth happens not in pews, but in the front seat of a car with nowhere to go but up.

# CHAPTER 4

# The Yellow Footprints

*Finding Purpose Through Service - The*
*Marine Corps Years*

Some of the most defining moments in our lives don't announce themselves; they unfold. For me, this chapter marked one of those moments where God was clearly at work, even when I didn't fully see it.

Around the age of 14, my dad remarried. He had been married a few times, but this one was different. Her name was Jewel, and she quickly became one of the most important people in my life. She was young, kind, and worked hard to make life better, not just for my dad but for my sister and me as well.

Jewel stepped in where my father couldn't or wouldn't. While my dad didn't have a relationship with us, Jewel saw how much we were struggling and did everything she could to help. She even helped my mom when she could. Like my mom, Jewel made sure we had clothes to start school so that we looked good and felt confident. She never let us feel left out or forgotten.

She came from a strong Christian family. Her mother and father, both now passed, embraced me as their own.

Her mom became my grandmother. Her dad treated me like a grandson. That Christian foundation, though subtle at the time, gave me a sense of grounding that I didn't even realize I needed.

Jewel had a son, Justin, my half-brother, and I love him dearly. Today, we're closer than ever, a blessing I thank God for. Their marriage eventually ended, but my relationship with Jewel didn't. We lost touch for a few years during my hardest struggles.

But when my father passed away in 2017 during Hurricane Irma, unable to get help due to the storm, she and I reconnected deeply. She remarried a great man named Steve, who, to this day, treats me like a son. They've been there for me through good times and bad, and I am grateful beyond words.

Psalm 103:8 says, "The Lord is compassionate and gracious, slow to anger, abounding in love." Even in the midst of all that chaos and uncertainty, I could feel His hand guiding me through Jewel and her family.

During those later years after high school, I jumped around; I was still bouncing from one place to another, starting businesses, learning from experience, and struggling to stay afloat. In 1993, I opened a furniture business in Minneapolis and lived there for about 18 months. Isolated and on my own, I leaned more on prayer during that time than I had in years. It was a period of learning, about books, numbers, and business, but also survival and perseverance.

The furniture store was an interesting one. My buddy Charlie, whom I speak of throughout this book, had a business where he would run classified ads in the paper advertising brass beds and day beds. The ad would say, 'Queen bed with brass headboard, new still in box, $300.' And several variations to that for the daybed, etc.

The idea of the store was that you would have no retail storefront. It was running classified ads, and people would call, schedule an appointment, and meet you at the storage unit. No overhead and great margins. Charlie ended up selling or franchising the idea to about 20 people around the country, and he would set them up with the necessary inventory and location. They would pay him 10% of the sales each week. On average, you made about $100 a bed.

I told Charlie that I wanted to open one in Minneapolis, and that's what I did. I packed up everything into my car and left Florida. I did well, I was selling about 30 beds a week.

One of my closest friends, Mike, decided to do the same thing, and he opened one in Milwaukee, about three hours from Minneapolis. We kept in touch. Either I went there, or he came to Minneapolis. He was a Marine who had served in the Gulf War and had seen combat. That experience changed him, but we remained close. In many ways, his discipline and experience began to shape how I viewed life.

Before selling my Minneapolis location in early 1994 for 10% of the gross sales paid weekly, similar to how Charlie built his business, I went to Chicago to an importer of brass headboards, footboards, and daybeds. I worked it out so that I could get my inventory directly from the freight forwarder, cutting out the middleman. I ended up increasing my margin by 20%. I was also able to do that for Mike since he was right up the road from Chicago.

After selling the Minneapolis store, I moved again, this time to Oklahoma City in early 1994 to set up a new store.

A note on the freight forwarder I want to share is that I ended up convincing Charlie that he, too, should remove the middleman and the freight forwarder and bring the inventory directly from China. His network was selling a few containers a month. That's what he did, he went to China and began importing furniture directly. He ended up with numerous large furniture stores all over central Florida. In addition to the beds, he was bringing in high-end furniture that you would see at Havertys or similar for pennies on the dollar. He still has a few of those today.

There were many times I would be praying and asking the Lord to guide me in my decisions or my next move. Literally, it all came down to finding myself wanting more. Mike helped me move to Oklahoma City, and I was there for only six or seven months. I had no community, no network, and no roots. But during that time, something inside me began to shift.

I had started to cut back on drinking, even quitting entirely for several months. My father had been a functioning alcoholic, and I had seen what alcohol had done to him. I didn't want that life. A friend of mine, Charlie, who didn't drink because his father died from it, was a strong influence during that time. He was successful and carried himself with discipline. I respected him deeply.

Still, my life felt unsettled. After a short time in Oklahoma, I packed everything into a U-Haul again and moved to Indianapolis, trying one more time to find what I was missing. The businesses weren't necessarily failing, but my spirit was. I didn't know it yet, but the restlessness and the ache inside weren't about work or money. It was about my relationship with God.

Jeremiah 29:13 says, "You will seek me and find me when you seek me with all your heart." I didn't realize it then, but that's precisely what was happening, I was seeking something deeper, something real.

I was tired. Worn down. In mid 1994, I reached a turning point. I called Mike and said, "Listen, I've got to do something different with my life. I'm bored, I don't feel connected, I need a challenge, I need a change."

I walked into a recruiter's office and joined the United States Marine Corps.

My test scores on the ASVAB were high, in the 90s, and the recruiter wanted me to pursue a technical job. But I didn't like that. I wanted to serve in the infantry, like my friend Mike had. I wanted purpose. I wanted change.

At the time, I was living in Indianapolis, but I was determined to go to Parris Island, not San Diego. I took the recruiter to a Colts football game and had a conversation with him. I found out that because I was west of the Mississippi, they were going to send me to San Diego. But I wanted the legacy and heritage of Parris Island. I made my case, and they approved it. I was classified as a "legacy Marine" and would ship to Parris Island.

Shortly before I shipped out, I made a brief return to Florida. During that time, I was in a bad car accident with my sister and a close friend, Scott. I remember lying on the backboard in the ambulance, praying Scott and my sister were OK, Praying I would be OK, although, at that time, I certainly didn't feel that way. Praying this wouldn't prevent me from joining the Corps.

Psalm 28:7 says, "The Lord is my strength and my shield; my heart trusts in Him, and He helps me." Lying there on that backboard, I felt that strength and protection surrounding me.

Thankfully, I was cleared. Just a few days later, I was standing on the yellow footprints at Parris Island.

I was 26 years old. Older than most recruits. Older than some of the drill instructors. I had businesses under my belt. I'd lived on my own. I'd been broke. I'd slept in my car. I'd been lost. But now, I was ready for something more.

Standing on those yellow footprints, I prayed that this was what I needed, that it would change my life. And it did. It absolutely changed my life. Somewhere in the back of my mind, I think I might have prayed that this wasn't a mistake, probably about the time the drill instructors were yelling, "Get off the bus and Get on my Yellow Footprints,"

Boot camp was intense, but I can remember specifically the Sundays when we had a choice. We could stay in the barracks and get ourselves squared away, or we could go to church. I always chose the church. Worshipping alongside 600 other recruits and singing hymns in that small chapel was one of the most spiritually powerful moments of my life. It gave me the strength I needed to push forward.

Psalm 133:1 says, "How good and pleasant it is when God's people live together in unity!" Those Sunday services were exactly that, a taste of the unity and brotherhood I'd been searching for my whole life.

I remember thinking the first week wasn't so bad, until we hit "pickup day." That's when the complete chaos begins. Multiple drill instructors are yelling at once. The real training begins. But by then, I was already committed.

There was a moment early on when I cracked a smile. A drill instructor saw it and shouted, "Dicks! You think this is funny?" I responded with the only honest thing I could say: "Sir, this is the first time anyone's been yelling at me who wasn't asking me for money."

He had nothing to say after that. Neither did anyone else.

In another instance, it is a story I will never forget. In the Marine Corps, as I said, no phone calls. The only way you can get one is if you do something great in the eyes of your drill instructor, like knock out a fellow recruit in combat-hitting skills or something to that effect, and that is what I did.

One of my rack mates, DeJesus, was on a contract for Band, there really is such a thing, Marine Corps band referred to as the President's Own, and that is one of the hardest, most competitive contracts in the country to get. You have to be a great musician. He played the trumpet and, I am sure, went on to do great things in the Marine Corps. It's worth saying that in the Marine Corps, no matter what your job is (contract or MOS), you are a rifleman first, so band members would get deployed like all other Marines.

One late night on Parris Island, it was nearly dark; we were doing hand-to-hand combat. We often did that training in the dark to help memorize our motor skills for the training. We were doing a specific skill in which I put a leg sweep on DeJesus and knocked him out. I felt bad, but the drill instructor came by and said, "Great job, Dicks." For that, I got a call home.

I remember writing my mom early on asking her to get three-way calling, if you know what that is, it will date you; if not, it is an ancient way to add another person to a call.

So, when I made that call, I called my mother, but I asked her to call the guy I sold my business to in Minneapolis. She did, and I reminded him that I was going out of town for a few months, but he was supposed to be sending me my money orders to my mom, who was forwarding them to me via letter she would write me on Parris Island. That's it. I told my mom I loved her and hung up the phone.

What I didn't realize was that one of my drill instructors was behind me listening to my call, normal. But what he heard was me asking the guy where my check was. That spread pretty fast among the other drill instructors, and at mail call, the drill instructor would ask me, "Dicks, we get our check yet?" The drill instructors would say, "This Marine is hard; he gets a call home, and instead of calling his mom, he calls a guy who owes him money." That little call helped me through boot camp. I gained a lot of respect from the drill instructors; after all, I was probably bringing in more money a week than they were making.

I was different from the other recruits. I was older, more mature in some ways, less in others, but this was my mission. God had planned this for me, and I embraced it. My rack mate, on the opposite side from the Marine going into the Band, was a young kid, 17, who was turning 18 and had come from Rikers Island. He'd been involved in a manslaughter case, and the judge gave him a choice: go to prison or go to the Marine Corps. He chose the Marine Corps.

The Corps broke me down and then built me back up. I was older than some of the drill instructors, and I kept thinking, "This is pure brainwashing. They're not going to get me."

But I remember graduation day when I marched down the sidewalks for the family day, the day before graduation, and saw my father, Jewel, and my little brother. At that moment, I realized something profound: They got me. I was a Marine. And I was proud of it.

The Marine Corps gave me what I had been missing: structure, discipline, purpose, and a family. It was my version of college. It gave me the confidence to accomplish something and a network that would last a lifetime. To this day, I've countless Marine friends who've helped me grow, and I've helped them in return.

One of the most important lessons the Marine Corps taught me was the power of mental toughness rooted in faith. We had a saying: "Mind over matter, if you don't mind, it doesn't matter." But this wasn't just about willpower; it was about understanding that with God, country, and Corps, in that order, you could overcome anything.

Marines are taught that God always comes first. That foundation of faith gives you the strength to push through when everything else fails. Whether you're facing physical challenges, emotional struggles, or circumstances beyond your control, Mind over Matter; if you don't mind, it doesn't matter. That is what we heard in the Marine Corps.

I've carried this mindset throughout my life, but I've learned that the ultimate playbook isn't a military manual, it's the Bible. That's the playbook that never changes; the one source of truth you can always rely on. When the world around you shifts and nothing seems certain, God's Word remains constant.

The discipline to get up every morning, make your bed, say your prayers, and carry out the plan of the day: that foundation was laid in boot camp, but it's been strengthened by my walk with God. There's something powerful about starting each day, acknowledging that God is in control, even when circumstances seem overwhelming.

As for starting your day, making your bed might seem like a small thing, but it matters. As Admiral William H. McRaven said in his famous University of Texas commencement speech:

"If you make your bed every morning, you will have accomplished the first task of the day. It will give you a small sense of pride, and it will encourage you to take on another task and another, and another. By the end of the day, that one task will have turned into many completed tasks. Making your bed will also reinforce the fact that little things in life matter. If you can't do the little things right, you will never do the big things right. And, if by chance you have a miserable day, you will come home to a bed that is made, that you made, and a made bed gives you encouragement that tomorrow will be better. If you want to change the world, start off by making your bed."

That simple discipline sets everything else in motion and reminds you that you have control over how you respond to whatever comes your way. It's about taking responsibility for the small things so you can handle the big things when they come.

This Marine Corps mentality, grounded in faith, has served me through every challenge I've faced. When external circumstances threaten to steal your peace, when problems seem insurmountable, when you're tempted to worry about things outside your control, that's when you remember: mind over matter, with God's help. If you don't let the circumstances defeat your spirit, they don't have power over your future.

The Corps taught me mental toughness, but my faith taught me where that strength ultimately comes from.

But life after boot camp brought new challenges. I graduated and was assigned to the Reserves during what I often describe as the "Clinton years", not in terms of politics, but because the military was underfunded and undergoing a drawdown during that period. There wasn't much action or deployment. I attended infantry school at Camp Geiger on Camp Lejeune, after which I was assigned to various units, including Infantry, Amphibious Assault, and Motor Transport.

The structure and intensity of boot camp were behind me, and now I had to learn how to be a Marine in the civilian world. Even without deployment, the experience continued to shape me into a different person. The discipline was still there, but so was the freedom to make my own choices, and not all of them were good ones.

But the challenges continued. I hadn't had a drink in over six months, but the night I graduated, I found myself back in a bar. It's very difficult as a Marine not to drink, especially with other Marines. It began a rough couple of years that would follow. However, the foundation was laid. I was different. God had used all those struggles to bring me to that place. And He wasn't done yet.

The Marine Corps taught me that I could accomplish hard things and that I was stronger than I thought. It gave me a family I'd never had and standards I'd never held myself to. To this day, it is part of my identity and the foundation for many lasting relationships and a sense of purpose.

I came to understand that God places us in the exact position He wants us to be, even if we don't know why in the moment. Over the years, I've come to believe that I am doing what He wants me to do. He gives us choices. Sometimes, they're hard. Sometimes they don't make sense. But there's always a reason.

Philippians 1:6 says, "Being confident of this, that he who began a good work in you will carry it on to completion until the day of Christ Jesus."

The Marine Corps had given me structure and purpose, but I still had to learn how to live with both discipline and freedom. That's a lesson that would take me years to master and one that would require me to lean even more heavily on my faith.

In the next chapter, I'll discuss what came after the Marine Corps, including meeting the woman who would become my wife and how God continued to guide, shape, and challenge me.

Because the journey wasn't over, it was just beginning.

# CHAPTER 5
# New Beginnings

*Sobriety, Love, and Finding My Voice*

By this time, my life had begun to take a different course. I had spent more than a year on active duty in the Marine Corps, transitioning to the Reserves during what I often describe as the "Clinton years", a period when the military was underfunded and undergoing a drawdown. There wasn't much action or deployment, but the experience made me a different person.

I met great friends and built relationships that would last a lifetime. What I didn't know at the time was how the Marine Corps would continue to redefine my life and become part of who I am today.

Looking back now, I can see that God places us exactly where He wants us, even when we don't understand why in the moment. Over the years, I've come to believe that I am right where God wants me to be. Sometimes, I don't know why, but I am doing what God wants me to do. He gives me choices, and maybe they're not always the right choice at the time, but there's always a reason.

I remember being on the rifle range when a Primary Marksmanship Instructor walked up and asked, "Dicks, what's that under your cover? Is that gray hair?" I said, "Yes, sir, that's experience." He chuckled and walked on.

It was true, I was 26 years old and had already owned multiple businesses, been homeless, and learned how to survive when I was too proud to ask for help. I wouldn't be here today without my uncles, Uncle Jack, Aunt Linda, Uncle John, and Aunt Sharon, who were always there when I needed help the most, even when asking was embarrassing.

But even with that foundation, I was still struggling in some areas of my life. In 1997, I reached a defining moment that would change everything.

I was out on my motorcycle, drunk, when I got pulled over. I don't even know how I could stand up. The police officer saw my military ID and told me to go home and not get back on the road. I'm not sure if that was a blessing or a missed opportunity for intervention, but it scared me.

The very next day, I attended a Florida Gators game, Saturday, August 30, 1997, at 6 p.m., featuring Florida versus Southern Miss. I still have the ticket stub on my wall. That was the last time I ever had a drink.

I said to myself, "I can't continue to do this. I have to give something up to get ahead. I looked around, and it was an easy choice, I spent the most time and money in bars. Most importantly, I thought to myself, my father has a drinking problem. I've seen the destruction. I don't want to be part of it." I'd never had a DUI, and I didn't want one. I didn't want the horrific possibility of driving drunk and taking somebody else's life in a terrible accident. So, I made the decision: I'm just not going to drink anymore.

For the next six months, friends would come up to me: "Come on, James, you want a drink? Let me buy you a drink." And I'd say, "No, I don't want a drink." What I realized over those months was that my circle started to change quite drastically. I started meeting different people with different goals.

Proverbs 13:20 says, "Walk with the wise and become wise, for a companion of fools suffers harm." When I stopped drinking, my whole circle changed. I started meeting different people with different goals, and they began to make me better in ways I'd never experienced.

And that's when the number one thing that has changed my life to this day happened: I met my wife, Deb.

I had not been drinking for about six months when I met her at a jazz club in Tampa. We dated pretty quickly, had our first dinner, and just really connected. I was still young, still immature in many ways. Coming from being somebody who was always out drinking and partying, I probably hadn't evolved the way I should have at that age.

Deb and I dated for 3 or 4 months and then stopped. We would talk on occasion, and I was sick to my stomach with feelings for her; I knew something wasn't right without her in my life. I remember going to the U.S. Open in June '98 with my then-brother-in-law Gene; Deb was the only thing on my mind.

I remember praying and asking God if she was the one. During our time in San Fran, Gene and I had many conversations about life, marriage, and family; I was in Love with Deb, something I had little experience in. I felt she was the one, but I didn't know what to do next.

But God answered my prayers; I was at a Tampa Bay Lightning game, one of the last games of the season, and there she was, walking down the breezeway at the Lightning game. That was it. I knew right there, at that exact moment, that we were going to be married; this was the right time.

We reconnected, and on February 12, 1998, we got engaged in Lake Tahoe, two days before Valentine's Day. I proposed, she said yes, and we were married in May of 1999. That fast.

Ephesians 5:25-28 reminds us, "Husbands, love your wives, just as Christ loved the church and gave himself up for her... In this same way, husbands ought to love their wives as their own bodies. He who loves his wife loves himself." Meeting Deb and marrying her taught me what real love looks like and how to put family first.

This chapter is really about Deb because she became my foundation through the toughest times when I needed God most.

Deb had a good-paying job, but when our son James was born in 2000, we both felt that our kids should be with their mother rather than in daycare. I wanted her to be with our family, with my son, and that was super important to us. As a result, I faced increased pressure to pay the bills, and my business struggled.

We reached a point where we were living in a home I had bought to renovate in Avila, a high-end neighborhood. It wasn't the best financial situation for us, but it's all part of how we got here. My friend Charlie, the one who didn't drink, lived across the street.

I remember doing Bible studies with someone many people would know, Tony Dungy, who was the coach for the Buccaneers at that time. Tony had great faith and used to have men's Bible studies at his house on Wednesdays. I attended several of those, and that helped build the closeness I needed with God.

However, things continued to get harder and tougher. Deb and my marriage struggled many times, but we always found a way to keep it together. She is, and to this day remains, an amazing Christian woman. She is by far my better half and the one who has continued to help me grow in my Christian life.

I felt a lot of pressure and was struggling financially. I was struggling and running out of options. I took a job in Orlando with my uncle Jack's help, but we didn't have the money for a car, let alone a second car that would allow me to commute, two and a half hours each way to Orlando from North Tampa every day.

I remember my cousin, who was years younger than me, gave me her used Cavalier, which was an answer to a prayer. I would leave before the sun came up and come home after the sun went down, and I didn't see Deb or my son as much as I would have liked.

The defining moment came when my wife was driving that Cavalier with my son, and they got stranded on the interstate right in the middle of Tampa, not a safe area to be stranded. I said, "That's it. Something has to change. I've got to make a change for my family." So, we packed up and moved to Orlando, where my Uncle Jack was there to help.

Our daughter, Jacki, came in 2004 after we had settled in Orlando. Like all fathers and mothers, but me especially like all fathers, I prayed that my wife would be safe and healthy during childbirth and that our baby would be healthy. I can remember during Deb's pregnancy with James, I prayed every night, asking God to look out for her, keep her safe, and that our son would be born healthy.

Then the second baby comes, and it's not as scary as the first, but it still is. After the first, you have a little better idea of what's happening, but my daughter was no different, I was praying to God that Jacki would be a healthy baby. And she was.

But my wife, in the second delivery, after having the baby, became sick, and Jacki would not nurse. We were both scared and nervous, and both prayed. Come to find out that the doctor had left a sponge in my wife during the delivery. Deb became septic, and it was very serious. Luckily, we got Deb back to the hospital quickly, and she had surgery to remove the sponge.

It is in those times that you pray a little more, a little harder. It's the other times that you need to remember that prayer should be a part of your life every day, not just when you need it.

While I was building my relationship with Deb and our family, I had been working in the Tampa-St. Pete real estate market with a business I founded called Affordable Homes Unlimited. I bought my first house in 1996 while still in the Marine Corps Reserves.

I met a man named Bob Reynolds, who would go on to become one of my dearest friends, someone that I often spoke about my sobriety with. He also did not drink, but he was a man of deep faith with whom I could always have meaningful conversations about life and faith.

When we first moved to Orlando, we lived in a nice townhome in Maitland, right across the street from Maitland Little League. We lived there for about a year and a half, then moved to Alaqua Lakes, where Bob helped me find a home, and we lived there for a few years. Then we moved again in 2003 to Alaqua, where we live now, Bob again helped us find the house. We have been there for more than 20 years. It is home, and we love it.

I first met Bob in the mid-1990s after answering an ad in the newspaper about buying homes. That first meeting changed everything. I bought my first property from him, a small flip where we painted and added carpet, and made a $25,000 profit. That was the beginning.

The following year, we bought sixty-seven homes. Then came apartment complexes, vacant land, and eventually millions of dollars in real estate deals. Through it all, Bob was my go-to realtor, business partner, and friend. We bought and sold hundreds of properties together.

Affordable Homes hit the late 90s, about the time Deb and I were dating, and the real estate market hit some tough times. By that time, I had bought and sold some 60 homes and had another 30 or so in inventory. I had transitioned from single-family homes to small apartments in St. Petersburg, where I owned approximately 200 rental units throughout the city. Bob Reynolds represented me in all those transactions.

The problem was that the market abruptly changed, and lending stopped overnight. I was over-leveraged and learned my first lesson on leverage and risk aversion. I was unable to sustain the business with no sales, and ultimately, I had to close the company and work out deals with all the banks. It was a very tough time financially, which put strains on my marriage, but Deb has always believed in me and supported me from day one.

Bob and I's friendship was more than real estate. Bob was a man of tremendous spiritual depth. We would sit for hours talking on the phone about God, faith, life, and our struggles. I was still drinking back then when I first met him, still figuring out who I was after the Corps. Bob always had a calming spirit. I could feel God working through him when we talked.

Bob was instrumental in helping me maintain my faith and believe that God had a plan for me, which led me to take a new job in Orlando with my uncle, Jack, and start traveling more. When I got married, when I had children, when I moved to Orlando, Bob was there. He helped me find the house my family still lives in today.

I remember when we bought our house in Alaqua; Bob bought us a huge centerpiece of flowers for our dining room table as a housewarming gift to say thank you and wish us much happiness in our new house. It was such a thoughtful gesture that showed the kind of man he was. Even when my business took off, and we talked less frequently, our connection was never broken.

In 2009, Bob recorded a testimonial for a real estate infomercial I did. In it, he called himself my "personal realtor" and reflected on the years we worked together. He said, "I'm Bob Reynolds, and I'm James Dicks's realtor. About twelve years ago, James answered one of my ads in the newspaper, and I went to see him. He was straight out of the Marine Corps, and we became fast friends, and I sold him his first house. The first thing that I notice about James is he's one who never gives up, and tenacity is a requirement in real estate. But the most important thing is to take the first step. And I think the thing that sets James Dicks apart from anyone else is his enthusiasm for the deal. It's infectious, and it gets you motivated to take the first step. I know that James has a heart to help people. He wants to see people succeed and to make their dreams come true."

I'll never forget his words or how genuinely proud he was of our journey. Bob passed away in February 2017, and it saddened me deeply. I know he struggled with his health, and we spoke a few times during that period. Even in those hard times, his faith never wavered.

Bob once sent me a manuscript, a work he had spent years laboring over. It was his spiritual interpretation of the Book of Revelation, the culmination of decades of study and prayer. At the time, I read parts of it but never fully absorbed it. As I was writing this book, I was reminded of Bob's manuscript. I went back to it and read through it. And I knew, without a doubt, that it needed to be published.

Bob was an interesting man, and I learned a great deal from him, both in real estate and in faith. It is my great honor to publish his book in memory of my friend. My prayer is that his words will continue to lead others into a deeper walk with the Lord, just as he led me.

Proverbs 27:17 says, "As iron sharpens iron, so one person sharpens another." Bob Reynolds was that kind of friend to me, someone God placed in my life to sharpen me both in business and in faith during some of my most formative years.

After the real estate business closed and with Bob's encouragement about God's plan for me, I started traveling more, doing training and educational events all over the United States. The travel started years earlier when I was fresh out of high school and had returned from Vermont. I went to work for my uncle John as a road crew, traveling the country with him as he was a platform sales speaker. That's when he got me on stage and taught me how to speak.

I can remember one time in Chicago at the McCormick Center, one of the largest convention centers in the United States. We were in a theater that holds 4,000 people, featuring a 10-foot-high stage and an orchestra pit below. I'm up there saying, "Good afternoon," trying to introduce my uncle, and I lost it; I was so scared I almost fell off the stage. I told everybody, "Can I start over again?" And I started over with "Good afternoon."

But those experiences taught me. My uncle taught me about various financial strategies, and with the confidence I gained from my uncle's teachings, I was able to ask a wide range of questions from groups of as many as 3,000 people. I'd be in the back of the room answering all types of questions. Ultimately, that turned into my ability to speak in front of people. I've talked to over 500,000 people worldwide on various topics.

That led to being on stage with some amazing people. I traveled on a lecture circuit where Colin Powell or General Schwarzkopf would speak before me. I remember one time in Memphis, Tennessee, I was speaking, and Zig Ziglar was one of the keynote speakers, an amazing motivational speaker and a man of faith. We were standing in line for lunch before the event, and I looked next to me, and it was Zig Ziglar. I just said, "Sir, would you care to have lunch?" So, Zig and I sat down and had lunch, just the two of us.

He taught me some incredible things. I remember one thing he told me: he would give the same presentation over and over, but he would spend two hours before every presentation looking in the mirror and going over it because he thought he owed it to the audience to be as good as he could be. That always stuck with me.

But what I learned was that my approach to speaking is different. I know my material; I go through it mentally, but in the end, it's always been, and always will be, that I say what God wants me to say. I feel like it comes out that way. If it's going to be great, it's because God wanted it to be great. If I say certain things, it's because God wanted me to say them, because I was meant to touch somebody in the audience.

1 Corinthians 2:4 says, "My message and my preaching were not with wise and persuasive words but with a demonstration of the Spirit's power." When I walk out on stage, I know that I'm going to do and say what God wants me to do and say. I have no fear of speaking, and I don't worry about whether it will be good or great. It's the way God wants it to be. I always say a prayer and ask God to help me do good and that my message will connect with people in the audience.

This approach to speaking was a huge defining moment in understanding how God uses us when we surrender to His will.

Getting sober, marrying Deb, and building our family - all of that was preparing me for what God had planned next.

Today, my wife, Deb, my daughter, Jacki, and my son, James, we have a great family. My wife is my rock, my better half, and the stronger component in our faith-based relationship and marriage. I learn from her every single day.

We're blessed that my son was able to attend a Christian school, and he has grown up to be a great Christian man who now works full-time with me in our development business. He's faith-based and motivating, and he brings the love of Christ to our family. I see that same foundation growing in my daughter, who is four years younger than my son. She is becoming an amazing young woman.

Sometimes, the greatest blessings come disguised as the greatest challenges.

In the next chapter, we'll explore how God continued to shape my path and calling in ways I never could have imagined.

# CHAPTER 6

# Finding My Purpose

## *Writing, Speaking, and Giving Back*

At this point in my life, things were starting to move along. We're talking about the late '90s and early 2000s, and things weren't as hard. I had started a new business, building on my stockbroker experience that I took with me into the Marine Corps. I started a business ultimately called PremiereTrade, but before I got there, I was speaking on the road for a company called WizeTrade and ended up creating a company called Forex Made Easy.

From where I was to where I am today, everything has grown, which in turn has allowed me to start giving back. That certainly doesn't mean I made millions and millions, though I always tell people that I made my first million by the time I was 30 and lost it by 31. That was a good year, but what I learned was that making it is easy and keeping it is hard.

One of the reasons why I felt that God had put all these experiences in my life was to share with other people who are struggling in some form or fashion. I believe God is using me as a means to communicate and connect with others. I don't understand it other than that's what God has in my life. And it's going to be even bigger as I continue to grow in my faith.

Specifically, in building PremiereTrade, it started with a book called "Forex Made Easy." As an experienced trader, I use different systems. My good friend George Thompson, founder of WizeTrade, had an algorithm that I adapted and used to create Forex Made Easy. I was in the right place at the right time; I was where God wanted me to be.

I was speaking with someone from McGraw-Hill, the world's largest publisher, about Forex trading and my idea for a book. Most people had never even heard of Forex and didn't know what it was. The market didn't open up to the masses until late 1998 into 1999. In late 1998, I did my first presentation on Forex in Vancouver, Canada. That's where it all started. There weren't many people there, but I learned a lot and was able to apply that knowledge into the early 2000s.

I remember McGraw-Hill saying, "Yeah, you write it, and we'll publish it. We like it. If you sell 3,000 copies, it's a success." So, I did. Long story short, that book is still on bookshelves today. It's in its 26th printing, with over 250,000 copies sold worldwide and translated into five languages.

It's unbelievable because when I wrote it, I had no support from McGraw-Hill. They just said, "Write it." I remember the grammar wasn't good. There were errors, misspellings, and all kinds of formatting issues. Over the years, I tried to get them to let me create a new version, but they wouldn't. They did let me go through it and update all the spelling and grammar, but I never rewrote the book. The book has only one or two chapters that are still relevant. The rest is outdated, but it serves as a foundation. People love it, and they still buy it.

But what that did for me was put me at a level of confidence that said, "Hey, here's somebody that struggled in high school, struggled in English, failed English, and maybe there's something there. Maybe I have something to give back." We won't even talk about math, but I can say that all those general math classes ended up being exactly what I needed in business all these years later. I guess God knew then what I would know many years later.

1 Corinthians 1:27 says, "But God chose the foolish things of the world to shame the wise; God chose the weak things of the world to shame the strong." Here I was, someone who had struggled academically, yet God was using my simple way of explaining complex topics to reach people.

I started teaching people through my writing. What I learned was I write and speak in a more simplistic way than most people. The average person in America reads at a level equivalent to an eighth or ninth grade, so the way I teach is something the majority of people can understand. That ultimately led to eleven books on various financial-related topics.

I think, yet again, God knew then that I would be writing this book today, and those skills have surely helped me share some of these stories about how I apply my Christian faith and how God has led me to this point.

This success with my first book opened doors I never expected. One specific book that really changed everything was called "Operation Financial Freedom." Interestingly enough, that wasn't my title, that was McGraw-Hill's title. The story behind that book takes me back to when I was in the Marine Corps.

When I was in the Marine Corps, I was already a stockbroker with all my financial licenses, and I specifically remember leadership, the company's first sergeant and the company commander. As a recruit, you don't want to see them. I used to be scared to death of running into them.

But I remember the company commander summoned me to his office. That's very unusual, maybe the whole time I was there, nobody else got that, and I was like, "Oh man, I messed something up. What did I do?" I remember going into his office and centering myself, and him saying, "Hey, at ease. So, I hear you're a stockbroker."

I was relieved with a smile, okay, this is probably something I can answer. We ended up having a good conversation. The CO told me he was getting a Harrier slot, was going to be a Harrier pilot, had already been investing, and wanted to run some things by me. Of course, I told him

I couldn't give specific investment recommendations, but we could discuss them in general terms.

At that point, I realized, "Well, hey, maybe I did have something to give back."

When we graduated, one of the courses we had to do at the end of boot camp was a financial class. Everybody was getting a check for around $3,000, which is a substantial amount of money, especially when you're 17 years old, as some of the recruits were. The financial class we were being taught was how to balance your checkbook, and I thought that was ridiculous. I thought it was a waste of an audience and a waste of young minds, especially when you have huge problems within the military with financial independence and education.

So, I wrote a book called "The Financial Guidebook for Marines." My publisher, McGraw-Hill, said, "Hey, we love it. We want to take it mainstream. We want to talk about all the branches and share these financial strategies." These were basic strategies, including the rule of 72, compounding interest, finding reasonable interest rates, investing in the stock market, IRAs, and investing in real estate. They wanted to add military quotes for motivation.

I was reluctant because that's not why I wrote the book. I wrote it specifically for Marines to help them get ahead. But I went ahead and did it. The book was released, but it didn't sell very well. But that's okay because what the book did was get me to the next chapter of my life, wanting to share those strategies with those in the Marine Corps.

The book caught the attention of the 15th Sergeant Major of the Marine Corps, John Estrada. I ended up meeting him in Washington, D.C., and we became good friends. He loved the book, loved the content, and thought his Marines needed it, so he invited me to attend his sergeant major symposiums with his command sergeant majors from all over the Marine Corps.

Those briefs led to meetings with other notable individuals, including the Master Chief Petty Officer of the Navy, the Master Chief Petty Officer of the Coast Guard, and the Sergeant Major of the Army. I established relationships with all of them and taught those same strategies to them and their sergeant majors, all of whom were enlisted personnel.

What that allowed me to do was build relationships with those sergeant majors. Some went on to carry big responsibilities at major commands, so I spoke to many enlisted across the branches in various situations all over the world, on aircraft carriers, different bases, and commands.

It was always amusing because, as I spoke to the enlisted Marines, soldiers, sailors, airmen, and guardsmen, an officer would always be standing in the back of the room, taking notes and watching. Everybody knew they had more money, got paid more, and went to college, but they always wanted to know more. That relationship began to develop with those types of people in the command structure.

What was amazing was being able to share that information. One of the biggest things we taught was about these young service members who started getting money working for the military. They don't have many expenses, but you often see new Mustangs driving around on base. These young service members were buying these cars with no money, so on Saturdays, they'd be out there washing and waxing them because they didn't have money to drive them.

You'd talk to service members, and they'd tell you their credit was terrible, how do they get ahead? They were enamored by this Marine who was enlisted, had this big business, wrote all these books, and they'd think, "Hey, maybe there's something out there for me. Maybe I can be successful."

I enjoyed sharing all of that. It came down to just sharing information with the service members and letting them know, "Listen, there were times in my life when I had the worst credit ever. I was paying 18% interest on my real estate loans and five points to close them, and I probably made more money during those tough times than I had ever before. Anybody can do it. If this Lance Corporal can do it, anybody can do it."

Philippians 4:13 says, "I can do all this through him who gives me strength." That became my message to these young service members, that with God's strength and the right financial strategies, they could overcome any obstacle.

I have tons of people coming up to send me emails. I'd follow up with them, and to this day, I have some amazing relationships. I became close friends with the Sergeant Major of the Army, Ken Preston, who served in that role for six years. He invited me to many of his training events and also invited me to Fort Bliss in Texas, where the Sergeant Major Academy is located.

That Sergeant Major Academy is the E9 school for all branches. They send their E9s, Master Chiefs, Command Sergeant Majors, Sergeant Majors, and Master Gunnery Sergeants, to learn that billet. At one time, I got up there, and I remember I was scared to death. I'd been telling jokes to Marines that made them laugh, and I was afraid I'd make the same jokes to the Army, only to find that they wouldn't laugh.

Of course, it went over great. It was one of those things where I just had faith in the Lord that I'd get up there and do my presentation, and it was what God wanted me to do and talk about and say.

I recall a presentation at Fort Bliss where six previous Sergeant Majors of the Army were in the room, and I became friends with many of them. That was a period in my life that, to this day, continues with my support for the military.

One of those sergeant majors became the Reserve Affairs Sergeant Major, so I did a lot of work with him. Another good friend, Brian Battaglia, became the Senior Enlisted Advisor to the Chairman of the Joint Chiefs, that's the highest enlisted military person in all the military services. I ended up doing work with him because we had such a great relationship.

I remember back in 2011, the Pentagon was having huge problems with soldiers and airmen coming home and collecting unemployment compensation, living with their parents in basements. It was a rough time financially; they were making more money in their basement on unemployment than they were earning at work. We had to help resolve that, so I was doing special reporting with the Chairman of the Joint Chiefs Office.

That led to so many more opportunities. In 2008, I became involved with the Department of Defense's Employer Support for the Guard and Reserve office, and in the next chapter, we'll discuss how it has led me to where I am today. I'm still doing work with that organization.

All this military outreach work also connected me with people who would become lifelong friends and business partners. One of the most important relationships during this period was with Jack Lott, who became not just a business partner but a dear friend and father figure. I met Jack in the early 2000s when he was working with the Business Talk Radio Network. We wanted to start doing a radio show, so I went down to the radio station and met Jack. They assigned him as my co-host, and together we created the James Dicks Financial Radio Network.

We would take calls from people asking about the markets, specifically, their stocks, foreign currency, or whatever they wanted to discuss. We'd input their information into PremiereTrade and tell them what we would do if we owned it. Of course, we couldn't give specific investment recommendations, but we could share our analysis and approach.

But the real story is about Jack Lott himself. Jack is an amazing man with an incredible history of service and faith. His media career began as a radio broadcaster in Cape Canaveral, Florida, in 1968, and he was a member of the Armed Forces Radio and Television Service for the U.S. Air Force. He served in Southeast Asia, Spain, Greece, and Greenland, literally like the "Good Morning Vietnam" guy during that era.

Jack spent nearly a decade on the academic staff at the U.S. Air Force Academy in Colorado Springs, serving as Director of Academic Television Production and Deputy Director of Visual Information Technology before retiring from the Air Force in 1990. After his military service, he became the Program Director of the Business Radio Network and later served as Senior Vice President of Operations and Programming.

Jack was with me through the entire PremiereTrade journey, from around 2002 to 2008. He became my Director of Communications, responsible for our creative marketing, audio/visual production, and innovative media strategies. But more than that, he was someone I would sit down with on a daily basis to get advice from. We'd discuss theology, God, business, life, and families. Jack was instrumental in many opportunities, including helping set up the trip where I flew with the Blue Angels.

After our radio show, we launched the James Dicks Financial Magazine, which was distributed to approximately 50,000 people per month. Jack wrote many articles for the magazine, but one of the most impactful was called "Preserve, Protect, and Defend" (PPD). It was an idea that Jack and I developed together, honoring those in service, much like the themes we've discussed throughout this book about serving others.

Colossians 3:23-24 says, "Whatever you do, work at it with all your heart, as working for the Lord, not for human masters, since you know that you will receive an inheritance from the Lord as a reward. It is the Lord Christ you are serving." This verse speaks to me and will be my approach to every speaking engagement, every documentary project, and every opportunity to serve our military families.

Jack would interview amazing people for our cover stories, and the magazine was very successful for four or five years. A lot of the content was based on things I would go out and do, and Jack would write about them, anything related to service or the military. We eventually took this concept to the next level with a production company we called Preserve, Protect, and Defend.

Jack's wife Judy had passed away after a long battle with health problems, and later, Jack met a longtime friend who became his new wife. He married Pat Jarrell Lott on February 24, 2017, and they've been happily married since. Jack is in his 70s and still sounds as young as he was the day I met him. We still talk regularly, and I'm grateful for the father figure he became in my life during those crucial business years.

Jack was awarded the prestigious Department of Defense Thomas Jefferson Award for broadcast excellence and the Quiet Leader Award from the Department of Homeland Security, as well as numerous military decorations. After our time together, he took a position as a public affairs officer for Homeland Security and the Border Patrol to complete additional years of service for his retirement.

Through my Uncle Jack, I also met Nick Nanton, who would become another important relationship during this time. Nick had attended school with my nieces and was a University of Florida graduate working on his law degree when he joined PremiereTrade's legal team. He and I became good friends and built a great relationship over the years, working on cash flow strategies when the company was struggling.

Nick went on to become incredibly successful, winning over 20 Emmy Awards for his work as a director and producer. He writes music, spends time in Nashville, and has done excellent film and television projects. His documentary work served as the foundation for the feature film "The Sound of Freedom," and he retains the rights to the sequel.

Years later, when I was working on marketing projects with DNA Pulse, I had an encounter that would reconnect me with Nick in a meaningful way. Sergeant Major Brian Battaglia, who we talked about earlier as the Senior Enlisted Advisor to the Chairman of the Joint Chiefs, came to me when he was getting ready to retire. He wanted to introduce me to Shari Duval, who we all lovingly called "Mom."

Shari founded K9s For Warriors in 2011 after her son Brett, a civilian K9 police bomb dog handler who served in Iraq, came home with PTSD. She realized he was only himself when with his dog. Doctors couldn't help her son, but she found that a service dog could. Shari found a new mission in life: to dedicate all her time and resources to helping restore the lives of her son and returning combat veterans through the use of service dogs.

We went up to see what this place was all about, and I met Shari and her team. It was incredible, the work they did, the training they provided for these dogs, the military veterans they brought in, and the love they showed them. K9s For Warriors serves our veterans as honorably as they served their country. Their lifelong program is provided to warriors at no cost and is designed to deliver maximum benefit with minimum administrative costs. All the dogs they use have been rescued from shelters, making it a beautiful story of second chances for both the veterans and the animals.

What started with Shari's own money grew into the largest service dog program for veterans in the United States. Sadly, we lost Shari in February 2021 after a courageous battle against cancer. Her legacy continues to shine with every veteran and rescue dog life saved by K9s For Warriors.

Their work so moved me that I got involved and told Nick, "Listen, I think this is a story for an Emmy. Let's go get an Emmy, it's a documentary." Interestingly, Shari's older son is David Duval, the professional golfer who spent many years competing with Tiger Woods.

We decided this was a great story, so we went out and raised the money, it costs three to five hundred thousand dollars to shoot a really good documentary. We shot "A New Leash on Life: The K9s for Warriors Story," and it turned out amazing, featuring incredible stories from veterans. We told their story on the big screen, and ultimately, it was nominated for numerous Emmys and won several Emmy Awards.

Later, I was doing a boss lift at Tyndall Air Force Base when the lieutenant colonel I was with introduced me to a young major named Dan Rooney. He's now a lieutenant colonel in the Air Force Reserve and an F-16 fighter pilot in the Oklahoma Air National Guard. Dan had founded an organization called Folds of Honor, and because I had worked with Shari, he and I knew the same people and hit it off.

Dan's story began on his flight home from his second tour of duty in Iraq. As his flight landed, the pilot announced they carried the remains of Corporal Brock Bucklin on board. Dan watched as Corporal Bucklin's twin brother walked somberly alongside the flag-covered casket to meet his family on the tarmac. Among them was the deceased corporal's young son, Jacob. Since that night, Dan committed his life to rallying patriotic Americans and meeting sacrifice with hope through Folds of Honor.

I called Nick and said, "This is an amazing story, Folds of Honor and the work they're doing, raising money to help children and spouses of fallen or disabled soldiers, airmen, Marines, and guardsmen continue their education. I think we should do a documentary."

Since 2007, Folds of Honor has provided life-changing scholarships to the spouses and children of America's fallen or disabled military, and now their mission extends to the families of first responders. They've awarded nearly 62,000 educational scholarships, with 45 percent going to minorities, making their recipient family as diverse as the country we call home.

We put together the documentary, raised the money, and went out to Tulsa to the Patriot Golf Course to shoot it. What started as an operation above Dan's garage in Oklahoma had grown into an organization that has raised over $100 million to provide educational opportunities for military families.

"Folds of Honor" came out fantastic and was nominated for multiple Emmys. During the production, I shared my perspective as someone who served in the Marine Corps, knowing how important it is for service members to have the peace of mind that their families would be taken care of. As I said during filming, "Most Americans don't realize that less than one percent of the public serve, and of that, half are Guard and Reserve. When you leave your family at home, that's the hard part. Organizations like Folds of Honor provide that safety net, ensuring that if something happens to you, your family members will have the opportunity for higher education."

Nick and I are still close, we get together every few months to talk about business and life. Nick is someone I feel came into my life for a reason. I helped him learn many things during the PremiereTrade days, and since then, I've learned many things from him as well. It's that student-becomes-the-teacher dynamic.

Both documentary projects were rooted in faith and Christian values. Shari Duval and Dan Rooney both operate their organizations with deep faith foundations, and it was a period when we were doing a lot of outreach and meaningful work together. What started as business relationships evolved into opportunities to tell stories that matter and serve causes greater than ourselves.

Psalm 78:4 says, "We will not hide them from their descendants; we will tell the next generation the praiseworthy deeds of the Lord, his power, and the wonders he has done." This verse perfectly captures what we were doing with these documentaries, telling the stories of modern-day heroes and the praiseworthy deeds being done through organizations like K9s For Warriors and Folds of Honor.

What started as a simple desire to help Marines with their finances had grown into something much bigger. God was showing me that He had a purpose for every struggle I'd been through, and He was just getting started with what He had planned for my life.

In the next chapter, we'll explore how this calling to serve others continued to grow and take new directions that would surprise even me.

# CHAPTER 7

# Serving My Country

*ESGR and Learning to Trust God's Plan*

As we left off in the last chapter, discussing financial freedom and military service, this chapter focuses on how those experiences led to my involvement with ESGR, Employer Support of the Guard and Reserve.

I became involved with the Department of Defense's ESGR in 2008, drawn to its mission. ESGR was started in 1972 on the heels of the Vietnam War when veterans were struggling to keep jobs or get hired after returning from service. ESGR formed a three-legged approach: ombudsman services, military outreach, and employer outreach.

The ombudsman services leg is where trained volunteers work with employers and service members to resolve conflicts related to the Uniformed Services Employment and Reemployment Rights Act (USERRA). If not resolved within 72 hours, the matter will be referred to the Department of Labor. The average ESGR success rate is around 74%.

The employer outreach leg, my favorite, involves educating and recognizing employers, often taking them to military facilities through events like boss lifts. You'd be surprised how many employers think their Guard members are just "out there camping." They don't realize what leadership roles they have and what great leaders they have access to.

I often take employers on an air refueling mission with the 927th out of MacDill Air Force Base in Tampa. I'll put these employees on a KC-135, and we'll refuel fighter jets.

A 19-year-old airman is lying down in the bottom of this aircraft, air refueling F-22s, multimillion-dollar jets. This person has a job working for their employer at a warehouse, where they're not even allowed to operate a forklift because their employer does not think they have enough experience; they're too young and not mature enough.

But I seat their employer right next to them when a fighter jet at 400 miles an hour comes up and pulls right behind us, 15 feet from the plane. They're looking at the pilot, waving, while their airman is sitting there, moving the boom and taking control of the flight operation.

When we landed, the employer stepped off the plane and said, "Wow, I had no idea, light bulb moment. I can't believe that. When we get back, my employee and I are going to sit down and have a conversation. They're getting a raise, and they're going to have a lot more responsibility in my office."

That's always been my favorite part of the experience for employers and their service members.

Many of the missions we conduct involve the Guard and Reserve, and when we conduct boss lifts with employers, there are numerous opportunities. I have felt strongly about, maybe God has put me in that position to make those connections.

I tell those service members, "This is an amazing opportunity for you. We have all these CEOs from big companies here to see what you do. I encourage you to talk to them, have a conversation, and ask them what they do. You never know what conversation you have that will get you a job or a career."

I tell the employers the same thing: "Talk to these service members, get to know them, ask them about their families, what they do, what they like, where they live. You never know, you might find your next corporate leader."

I have witnessed many conversations lead to successful outcomes, and numerous service members secure amazing jobs. One such job was that of an airman, Xavier, who was part of the PAO staff or Public Affairs Office. We got to be good friends, and on one flight, I was with Trevor Gooby, who was a VP in the Pittsburgh Pirates organization involved with player development.

He was involved in the story of "Million Dollar Arm," where they went to India and found a pitcher, a great inspirational movie. Trevor is now the facility manager for the Seattle Mariners.

Trevor was on an air refueling mission, and I was able to introduce the two of them. Xavier ended up getting a marketing job with the Pirates organization. Every time I see one of those connections, I know I was there, doing what I was doing by the grace of God and helping others in an impactful way.

In 2015, I was appointed State Chair for ESGR Florida by the Secretary of Defense, a position carrying a two-star general protocol. I had 120 volunteers and 11 staff. My job was to brief the adjutant general and governor on employer strength and reserve readiness. In Florida, there are 35,000-plus Guard and Reserve members at any one time, plus their family members.

What's important to note is that I always tell employers: "Listen, it's easy to be deployed downrange, three hot meals and a cot, carry out the plan of the day. However, the truly challenging aspect is that many of these reservists are high-paid individuals. Maybe they're engineers, and maybe they're doctors. When they go to do their service in the military, and keep in mind, less than 1% of the American public are serving at any one time, these Guard and Reserve members get paid significantly less than their civilian jobs. So, there's a deficit there."

Some employers will actually pay that difference, which is essential. And I always say, "Listen, the hard part is leaving your family at home. These are proud people. They won't ask for help. As an employer, I always told employers: "It's harder to leave your family than to go downrange. These proud men and women won't ask for help, go see if they need their grass cut or their lights turned on." That's always been an important mission to me.

Through ESGR, I established relationships nationwide and engaged in meaningful conversations with employers, service members, and leadership. It's through this ESGR platform that I've continued my outreach. I learned a lot and was able to carry on lessons from the past. I met amazing people through ESGR, and to this day, I'm still the boss lift coordinator and chair emeritus, which allows me to continue reaching out.

I would be in Washington, D.C., regularly, meeting with people just like me who had been appointed as state chairs, including Guam and Puerto Rico. I built some really good relationships and certainly learned a lot about how to continue my message and talk to the troops.

I recall visiting one of my units, 4th Amphibious Assault "Four Tracks" in Tampa, and speaking with those Marines where I once served. I shared my story and explained how they can continue to apply the leadership skills they're learning and that their employers are lucky to have them. I was able to speak with Marines in Tampa about their futures. As a once-young Marine Lance Corporal who now had a DOD appointment, I saw the incredible reach and responsibility God had led me to.

It's at this time that you look back and know that God has a plan for you. Here I am, a young kid, a young adult struggling, who goes into the Marine Corps, comes out of the Marine Corps as a Lance Corporal, and some years later is appointed to a position at a Department of Defense office, which carries a two-star major general protocol. It starts to increase that credibility.

Isaiah 55:11 says, "So is my word that goes out from my mouth: It will not return to me empty but will accomplish what I desire and achieve the purpose for which I sent it." Looking back on this appointment, I could see how God had been preparing me for this role through every struggle and every experience, and now He was using me to accomplish His purposes in the lives of military families.

What that increased credibility brings is the ability to capture a larger audience, to have a bigger audience, and to share more effectively. People listen to you more, and you're able to advance that message. As I continue to learn every single day, hence the writing of this book, where I share my deep-rooted faith, I know there's much more to discuss.

Now, managing all these responsibilities and the emotional weight of helping military families taught me one of the most significant lessons I've learned: the importance of compartmentalization. It's how I remove stress and worry. I picture problems as files in a cabinet. If I can't solve it today, I shut the drawer and don't revisit it until I can address it. I learned this through faith, service, and practice. When things were tough, I trusted that if God gave me breath in the morning, He had a plan for that day.

It's the Marine Corps, it's my faith, it's this job I had at the Department of Defense that allowed me to realize that you have to compartmentalize things in your life, which eliminates worry and stress. Not that I have a secret formula, but certainly, through what I've experienced, we've arrived at where we are today.

When I go to bed, I don't worry about things. I sleep fine. I don't think about anything specific to work or things that are going right or going wrong. I just know that if it's in God's plan for me to wake up in the morning and take a breath, there's a plan for me. I have to carry out that plan. Sometimes I know what it is, sometimes I don't, but I know God has a plan for me.

So, I don't worry about anything. Whatever happens is supposed to happen, and I just have to figure out what that means and how I can carry that forward and explain that to people.

What I mean by compartmentalization, and many people struggle with this, is that I like to look at problems like a file cabinet. You put stuff in your file cabinet, and you leave it there. You shut the file cabinet. If you're like most people, you never open it again. That should be the way you handle problems and situations.

If you can't solve it right now, today, if God doesn't give you that ability or doesn't give you that clarity you need to solve that specific problem, maybe it's paying a bill, maybe it's an electric bill, maybe it's a presentation, then you just put it back in, close the file cabinet, and pull something else out that you can solve today. You do not think about or worry about anything in the file cabinet unless you can fix it or do something about it today.

Matthew 6:34 says, "Therefore do not worry about tomorrow, for tomorrow will worry about itself. Each day has enough trouble of its own." This compartmentalization has become one of my core principles for managing stress and uncertainty.

I can't tell you how many times in the past when we were struggling, and I didn't know how I was going to pay the electric bill; I wouldn't worry about it. I'd wake up the next morning, and there'd be a check in the mail for something I didn't know about, or something would happen - maybe it was a phone call or a connection; you never knew, but you just knew God was working in your life. I just have that faith to know that there's going to be something there. Whether it's good, bad, or whether it's not there, you just have to continue to move on.

I've been homeless. I've counted change for gas and food. More than once, at the convenience store, buying a box of macaroni and cheese. But I've also run multimillion-dollar companies. One thing I learned is no matter how bad things get; you have to just get up. You have to just do something. I used to tell people who would listen, "If you're struggling, you've got to get out of bed." Even if you get up and wash the windows, mow the grass, make a call, it's that movement, that conscious action that spawns the next opportunity.

James 2:17 says, "Faith by itself, if it does not have works, is dead." Your action will strengthen your faith. I can remember one of the first early jobs my Uncle Jack gave me as a stockbroker was cold-calling people and raising money for a fund. I hated it. It was the worst thing ever. I was commuting from Plant City at that point, I was young, back in the early '80s, and I would drive two hours each way and just dread going and dread coming back.

Never did I realize that all of that was for a reason. Today, that's one of my specialties, I get on a phone call and have a conversation like I'm standing right in front of somebody. It serves me well. I used to cold call for hours. I hated it. However, I now realize that experience has shaped one of my strongest skills: connecting with people instantly. God knew. He had a plan.

That's why I want to remind readers that if you feel nudged to make a call or send a message, do it. That's God prompting you. Obedience in those moments can save someone's job, give someone hope, or even save a life.

So, people just need to understand that sometimes, when you're faced with despair, you just pick up the phone and make a call. Whether you're calling a hotline, a crisis line, or you're just calling a friend, it's that conversation that will spur, or that movement that will spur, the next thing you need in your life.

You've to have that faith and know that God is there and that maybe that phone call is the one. That one phone call is the one that's going to change your life. So, you just have to do it. You have to make it. I think that's where Nike got it right: "Just do it."

I've seen that work over and over for me. When things were tough or getting tough, I always would just pick up the phone and start calling people. By the end of the day, something had changed. Some opportunity had come up.

Proverbs 3:5-6 reminds us, "Trust in the Lord with all your heart and lean not on your own understanding; in all your ways submit to Him, and He will make your paths straight." That's been true in every chapter of my life.

This is how all the opportunities from the past led up to this great opportunity of working for the Department of Defense. It's this faith that enables you to continue moving forward. Then you've got to figure out how to give back.

For the Department of Defense job, my way of giving back was working with various employers and ensuring that Guard and Reservists had jobs when they returned home and that they could take care of their finances.

I believe the lessons of compartmentalization and "just do it" are among the reasons I'm writing this book. God has shown me that every experience, even the ones I hated at the time, was preparing me for something greater.

I did two three-year tours as the state chairman for ESGR. Typically, when your final tour concludes, you have a recognition ceremony at the Pentagon and receive tokens of appreciation from one of the secretaries. It's a big event, well-attended. I have been to many.

Unfortunately, I did not have that opportunity, as it was right in the middle of Covid, so no travel was allowed. However, I was awarded the recognition, and as with any award for service, it's the best recognition you can receive. Simple, but you feel the appreciation. You do not do what you do for the recognition or the award, it's simply a thank you.

The Secretary of Defense Medal for Outstanding Public Service is the second-highest award presented by the Secretary of Defense to non-career Federal employees, private citizens, and foreign nationals for contributions, assistance, or support to Department of Defense functions that are extensive enough to warrant recognition. Here is my citation:

Mr. James Dicks is recognized for exceptional public service as the State Chair of the Florida Committee for Employer Support of the Guard and Reserve, Defense Personnel and Family Support Center, Defense Human Resources Activity Office of the Under Secretary of Defense for Personnel and Readiness from October 2014 to September 2020. His exceptional leadership, dedication, and commitment to the mission of the Florida Committee significantly enhanced and sustained employer support for the men and women serving in the United States Armed Forces Guard and Reserve. Mr. Dicks' performance and initiative were the driving force behind significant improvements to the essential Employer Support of the Guard and Reserve programs of Employer Outreach, Military Outreach, and Ombudsman Services. Committing substantial personal time, he routinely went above and beyond the requirements of his position to support the mission of the Headquarters Employer Support of the Guard and Reserve, the Florida Committee, the thousands of Guardsmen and Reservists in Florida, and their supportive employers. As a result, employers have gained a greater understanding and appreciation of their employees' Reserve Component military service. The distinctive accomplishments of Mr. Dicks reflect great credit upon himself and the Department of Defense.

Reading that citation reminds me that none of this was really about me, it was about serving others and being faithful to the calling God had placed on my life.

Every struggle, every lesson learned, every skill developed was preparing me for this period of service.

In the next chapter, we will discuss some of the other ways God continued to open doors and expand my ability to serve others.

# CHAPTER 8

# Fellowship, Testimony, And The Church

*Finding My Spiritual Home*

In this chapter, let's talk about the role's churches have played in my walk with God, how different churches have influenced my spiritual foundation, even when I didn't realize it at the time.

As I mentioned in earlier chapters, I was exposed to churches from a young age, including Plant City Baptist Church, Plant City Methodist Church, and the First Baptist Church of Brandon. These early years weren't necessarily by my choosing, but they were vital in planting the seeds of faith. Over the years, I've also attended some Catholic masses for friends and family.

My good friend Mike, the Marine who lived in Milwaukee and Minneapolis with me and who was the inspiration behind my decision to join the Marine Corps, has a brother named Tom, who is a Catholic priest. It's an interesting story because when Mike went to the first Gulf War, his brother Tom signed up and joined the Navy to be a chaplain. He deployed and was a Navy chaplain for many years. He went on to be the priest at the Plant City Catholic Church, then at the church in Tampa, and ultimately became the priest at the Catholic Church in Lecanto, Citrus County, before returning to Tampa.

I attended my buddy Mike's wedding at the Catholic Church in Tampa, and I was also recently at Mike's mother's funeral at the same Catholic Church, which was beautiful and well-attended. Approximately 30 priests and two bishops were present. She was a great woman who led by example in her service and commitment to the church.

One of the most memorable church experiences I had was sometime in the early 2000s when I was in London speaking at a trading expo at the Queen Elizabeth Convention Center. Mike and I were at the event and decided to attend a Wednesday night service at Westminster Abbey, which was located right across the street. I am so glad we did. The story is amazing but just knowing you were in the church where so many kings and queens throughout time have been crowned, it was surreal. The choir was excellent, and the service was great. I enjoyed the experience of worshipping in such a historic place where centuries of Christian tradition had taken place.

However, for me, as an adult, church began in the late '80s when I was in Orlando working there for the first time. I was doing Bible studies with Buddy, and they were very good friends with Dr. Joel Hunter, who was the pastor of Northland, a non-denominational Christian Church in Castleberry. So, I started attending that church.

That church began as a small congregation in an old roller-skating rink, and I thoroughly enjoyed it. I enjoyed the music and the fellowship. It was not like the Baptist and Methodist churches that I was familiar with, but I loved the gospel, the singing, the worship, and the message. I had the opportunity to do that for a couple of years, and it helped shape my Christian life. Then life changed, I went to the Marine Corps and moved on, as you know from this book.

The next time I returned to that church was when Deb and I had moved to Orlando with my son, James. We started attending the church, and it was still in the same old roller skate rink. We became good friends with Duncan Jones, who was a friend from traveling. He ultimately married a young lady who was friends with my wife, so our families were close. I want to share a story with my good friend Duncan later in this chapter.

We attended the church and enjoyed it. Then, my son attended Methodist Church Pre-K and kindergarten, so we naturally gravitated toward the Methodist Church at that time. My daughter was born, and we would go to that church in Longwood. We ultimately made it our home church.

I had flashbacks to my days at Plant City Brandon Baptist Church and Methodist Church. I just didn't feel it. I didn't feel connected, but my son was going to school there, so it was good for him. At that point, my daughter and son were baptized, and I was baptized with them. It was the first time I had been baptized.

1 Peter 3:21 says, "And this water symbolizes baptism that now saves you also, not the removal of dirt from the body but the pledge of a clear conscience toward God. It saves you by the resurrection of Jesus Christ." Getting baptized with my children was a powerful symbol of our family's commitment to following Christ together.

Then we were at that church for a little while, but we were just missing something. By that time, the new church for Northland had been built. It's a big church, yes, you would call it a megachurch, and we started attending. I loved that church. I loved the pastor, Pastor Joel Hunter. I had connections with him back in the late '80s, and I just embraced it. I remember having a daddy-daughter dance there and attending a MercyMe concert there. It was a good time with the church at that point.

The church grew significantly, reaching 3,000 people per service. I recently attended a sermon with the pastor at my new church, where they discussed megachurches and how some people tend to view them with skepticism. However, his message was specifically about preaching from Acts and discussing how the very first church was a megachurch, I took the time to read the verse my pastor was referring to.

Acts 2:41 says, "Those who accepted his message were baptized, and about three thousand were added to their number that day." which describes the birth of the early church right after Peter preached on the day of Pentecost: Peter, filled with the Holy Spirit, gave a bold sermon about Jesus being the Messiah. The people were convicted and asked, "What shall we do?" Peter told them to repent and be baptized. This moment marks the beginning of the Christian church. It was a powerful move of God, showing how faith, the Holy Spirit, and bold Preaching could reach people in large numbers, forming one of the first "big churches" in history.

Churches were meant to be megachurches intended to spread the Word. After hearing the sermon, I gained a different perspective on big churches, as I know some people say, "Well, it's too big; maybe it should be smaller." But I like the big feeling. I like the worship. I like the praise.

I remember one time coming home from Washington, D.C., I traveled there quite regularly, as we talked about in other chapters. I was sitting in first class on the plane, having a conversation, when right next to me sat Pastor Joel Hunter on his way home. He was coming back from a meeting with the president, as he was on the board of the faith-based coalition. As usual, I respect people's privacy, but I talked to him for the entire trip, and we had some great fellowship. Interestingly, he knew my Uncle Jack, and he knew Buddy. There were just a lot of connections there. That was a highlight.

Pastor Hunter was particularly skilled at connecting worship services with everyday life lessons and problems that parishioners could relate to and understand. But he retired. When he retired, the new pastor came in, and we just didn't have the same connection. So we ended up not going to church and kind of lost our way with the church for a while.

Then, my son got married in 2023. He and his beautiful wife, my daughter-in-law Sarah, really started getting involved with church. They led a Bible study group and built some great relationships. The youth pastor there was a good friend of theirs and officiated at their wedding. They go to a church called Journey in Apopka.

My wife and I started going to it, and we enjoyed it. I recall one sermon where our former pastor, Joel Hunter, was the guest speaker; he had recently retired from Northland. It reminded me how much we missed his sermons., I got to go up and talk to Pastor Hunter, who remembered us and knew us. We liked the church and began attending regularly. Then, the pastor (John) retired, and a new one, Dustin, came in. Dustin was good, he's young, but we just didn't feel the connection anymore.

So, we ended up attending Lake Mary Church with Pastor Shaddy Soliman. I recall the first sermon we attended. I learned a great deal about the church, including its origins, which date back 15 years to when I began teaching at Lake Mary High School. They had about 15 people and started with a youth ministry for youth athletes at Lake Mary High School. It just grew to what it is today. They have just opened the new balcony section of their church, and it now accommodates 1,000 people per service.

I think the most prolific difference I noticed was that Pastor Shaddy taught a little differently than Pastor Dustin, and that's okay. Some of Dustin's sermons were truly inspiring, and I found them deeply meaningful.

But while researching this book and comparing and contrasting my last church to my new church, I have learned that my previous church pastor, Dustin, was more in line with Topical Preaching, which Focuses on a specific topic or life issue (e.g., marriage, anxiety, forgiveness) Pulls from multiple verses across the Bible to support the message Often uses stories, illustrations, or current events to relate to people. In contrast, my new pastor.

Pastor Shaddy is an expository preacher. Verse-by-verse or passage-by-passage explanation Focuses on the original context, meaning, and application of Scripture Stays rooted in one main biblical text at a time Goal: Teach the Bible as written, not just use it as a reference.

I feel my new pastor's teaching style was more in line with where my faith is, and As I have said already in the book, I felt like he has unlocked the next level of my faith and understanding.

The Lake Mary Church has that same great fellowship and singing that we like. We love the church, and we've already become friends with the pastor. We're starting to become more involved, and I feel that my relationship with God is growing stronger every single week. I'm so excited to go to church on Sunday.

Acts 2:46-47 says, "Every day they continued to meet together in the temple courts. They broke bread in their homes and ate together with glad and sincere hearts, praising God and enjoying the favor of all the people. And the Lord added to their number daily those who were being saved." That's what I see happening at Lake Mary Church and in our community.

An observation from the early 2000s: I recall when I attended Northland Church, I had a BlackBerry, and there was a website for the Bible, so I would pull it up and follow along with the pastor's sermon. It was great to follow along; you didn't need to pull out the Bible and find the verse; you just searched for it. I recall that there were not many people doing that at the time, and it was certainly frowned upon. So, I put it away.

Fast forward 20 years, and I realized that while sitting in church, as the pastor mentioned verses and read from Scripture, everyone in the church had a phone, and many were on it, taking notes. I'm sure not all were taking notes, but I found myself taking some as well. What a transformation from being discouraged from using technology in church to becoming an integral part of worship!

I am talking about how technology has become integrated into the church and how people use technology to become closer to God and build their faith. What does that mean? Well, using your phone to follow along in church with the Bible verses, taking notes, and maybe even using the Bible app to hear the Bible read to you while you're driving. Numerous apps will read Scripture to you throughout the year.

But look at churches today, especially some of the megachurches, technology is everywhere. Services are streamed live all over the world. People are watching and commenting in real-time. Churches often have their own apps for managing prayer requests, coordinating small groups, and registering for events. Online giving has made tithing and offerings more accessible than ever.

The pandemic accelerated this transformation dramatically. Suddenly, churches that had never considered streaming were reaching people across the globe. Virtual small groups connected believers across distances for Bible study and fellowship. Pastors were doing online counseling sessions and digital discipleship.

Consider the tools available today: Bible apps like YouVersion have reading plans and devotionals. Worship lyrics appear on screens instead of hymnals. Churches utilize social media platforms like Facebook, Instagram, and even

TikTok to connect with people. Podcast sermons enable people to listen to messages while commuting and during workouts. Digital discipleship programs offer online courses and virtual mentoring.

What I find amazing is that God uses all tools, even technology, to draw people closer to Him. The heart behind the BlackBerry in the early 2000s was the same as the iPhone today: a desire to engage more deeply with God's Word. Technology doesn't replace spiritual experiences; it can enhance them.

I've watched my own family embrace this. My wife uses a Bible app to listen to the Bible while driving. We use our phones to take notes during the sermon.

The key is intentionality. Technology can be a distraction, but it can also be a powerful tool for spiritual growth when used purposefully. Whether it's following along with Scripture, taking sermon notes, participating in online Bible studies, or connecting with believers around the world, technology has opened new avenues for worship and discipleship that our grandparents could never have imagined.

In 2008, I was training for the Marine Corps Marathon. A few things to know it takes about 450 miles of training on a 12-week schedule to prepare for a 26.2-mile marathon. I started in the summer preparing. I can remember training many times in pouring rain to get my miles in and stay on target.

One thing that was humorous was that I felt with all the training, maybe I could learn Spanish. I was running 5-6 hours a week, building to about 15 hours a week. So, I got a Spanish app for my phone, maybe Coffee Spanish. But it's pretty hard to jog and listen to how to say hello in Spanish, not too motivating for running. I didn't do that for long, although I did get a foundation of some basic words before I stopped.

I had to have something to listen to. Music was good, but I wanted constructive time management. To run a marathon is simple: mind over matter. I mention that in my Marine Corps years. The Marines taught me to set a goal and achieve it, being mission-driven. But you have to have some faith to know you can do it.

I decided to download Joel Osteen's first book, and that led to listening to all the ones he had available at the time. For me, it was an inspiration. I loved the stories and the motivation. My idea of crossing the finish line went from speaking Spanish fluently to preaching. In seriousness, I got a lot out of those books, and its funny how God's plan is always working. I spent all that time training for the marathon and continued to build my faith. Maybe not my walk with Christ, but certainly my jog with Christ.

I was well prepared for the marathon. But I was in Washington about two weeks before to run and acclimate to the course and weather. You see, I like to train in the middle of the day; the hottest times in Florida can be 100 degrees and 90% humidity. The Marine Corps Marathon is held in late October, and it can get cold.

Out on my first jog, about a mile into a 7-mile run, I pulled my calf. That was it. I had to walk back painfully to the hotel and come back to Florida. No more running. I had to train biking more than anything. I missed my last long 20-mile run, but there was no way after 450 miles; I was missing the marathon.

Late October, early morning, foggy and cold, about 38 degrees, far below anything I trained in. 4:00 AM, heading to the start line with patella straps on both knees and my tear-away tracksuit. So far, so good. The gun goes off, and so do I, feeling pretty good. I probably didn't stretch as much as I should have, and now it's here.

The first 7 miles are through Georgetown, and those who have been there know lots of hills, essentially all uphill for that section. I certainly did not train for that. At mile three, I tore my calf muscle: a loud pop and lots of pain.

No way was I stopping. It's the Marine Corps Marathon, the fog has lifted to blue skies, and 35,000 spectators. I cranked down my patella straps now on my calf and kept going. There was no way I was stopping, not with all the wounded warriors doing their thing. I finished in about 5 hours; 40 minutes longer than I would have finished without the injury. Oh, and I couldn't walk for two months.

And yes, did I say a prayer or two? I prayed the entire way to help me finish, to follow these motivational wounded warriors doing something great. I knew I could finish.

Fast forward to 2024. My niece decided she was going to run the Marine Corps Marathon. She put in the training and was super excited about it. She called and asked if her uncle would come, and she wanted her dad to come. Her dad had run it in 2005 and 2006. When you finish, you get a medal. So, she wanted him to bring his two medals, and she wanted me to bring my medal; she also wanted a picture of all three of us with our medals.

Deb and I went up there, and we walked about 16 miles in two days, sightseeing and following her in the marathon. And that was it. That's all it took. I knew it. I set a goal. I want to run the Marine Corps Marathon. The 50th anniversary is coming up in October 2025.

I decided I was going to start training for that. This was October 2024, at the end of the month. I had to get a few things straight. I had some issues with my back, my calf, my knees, and everything else. However, I knew I had to resolve all that. I started walking, then transitioned to a slight jog, increasing my miles and sticking to my plan.

And then, sometime in March, I had an accident in my garage where I was turning and completely dislocated my patella on my right knee. That pretty much put a halt to everything. I'm still having some issues with strained calf muscles on that right leg, which has plagued me ever since.

However, I am continuing to work through it now. I'm in June, and I have to decide whether I'm going or not. I've got to start building my miles. My goal is still to run the 50th-anniversary Marine Corps Marathon in October. It'll likely take some prayers along the way to get there, but I can. It's not easy, but great things aren't necessarily easy. It takes hard work.

What's interesting is we have some great neighbors that have been around for about four years now, Kristy and Doug. I personally owe a lot to my newfound closeness with God and my relationship with them. They have a Bible study once a month, and I attend that and enjoy it. I get so much out of it. The theme is that they have different people share their testimonials. Kristy has grown up with God, and their family is close to that. Her mother, Mimi, can recite the Bible, which is impressive to me every time I hear her speak. It draws me in to listen to the Word, and it has had a profound effect on me.

Ultimately, it is one of the driving forces behind me writing this book. The last few weeks of writing this book have been a spiritual journey. I have put in a lot of research while writing this, and I want people to know that if you keep your eyes open, there will always be opportunities to continue growing your faith.

There are people around you, and you just have to open your eyes and embrace them, having those conversations. Next thing you know, you're going to be in a Bible study with friends and family or new friends, and your opportunities are going to expand and grow. You're going to be able to share your experience and your testimony, and God is going to do great things in your life and use you the way He had planned from the day you were born.

Hebrews 10:24-25 says, "And let us consider how we may spur one another on toward love and good deeds, not giving up meeting together, as some are in the habit of doing, but encouraging one another, and all the more as you see the Day approaching." That is what church has become for me: a place of encouragement, growth, service, and worship.

What I've learned through all these different church experiences is that God meets us where we are. Sometimes, that's in a traditional Baptist church as a child; sometimes, it's in a converted roller rink; sometimes, it's in a megachurch; and sometimes, it's in a neighbor's living room. The building doesn't matter; it's about the heart and the community of believers.

God knew exactly what He was going to do in my life, and one of the things I will continue to share in the following chapters is my renewed faith-based journey, which I feel I was called to do. I want to continue sharing some of the stories from my life that will help others.

In the next chapter, I want to tell you about some friends and how God used me in their lives. I'll share stories about times I was able to help, and times I wish I'd done more. Those relationships shaped how I understand friendship and being there for others.

# CHAPTER 9

# Friends, Faith, And Intervention

*Divine Appointments in Relationships*

In Looking back, I can see how God puts the right people in our lives at just the right time. Some are there to help us. Some are there for us to help them. All of it is part of God's plan, and often, we don't understand it until much later.

There's Buddy, my uncle Jack's partner, who supported me in my early brokerage days at Delta First Financial. He and I had regular Bible studies, which helped me see how faith and finance could interact and, more importantly, that I was not alone.

Alongside him was Jim Paris, who worked there and started James L. Paris Financial Services. He was a faith-based Christian financial author and radio host who had his TV show. I remember working on that show and having conversations with Jim. He was instrumental in helping me grow my faith base in the late 1980s and early 1990s. His example showed me what it meant to be publicly and unapologetically Christian in a professional field.

Then there was Charlie. Charlie was the real inspiration behind my decision not to drink. He was a successful friend who had lost his father to alcoholism, and that motivated him to stop drinking early on and all through the '80s. His example helped me quit, too. We had some similarities, my dad had a drinking problem, too, and a lot of people took advantage of him. My father was drinking and had an accident in the middle of Hurricane Irma in 2017; he hit his head and passed away with nobody able to help him because there was no phone service and four feet of water from the storm.

Charlie and I have been connected through various life events. Unfortunately, I think I was the catalyst for him falling off the wagon, he stopped drinking, then started drinking again, which I've always felt bad about. But he realized that fairly quickly and stopped drinking probably two or three years before I did. That became one of my motivations: "Hey, my buddy Charlie did it again. I can do it." Charlie was able to recommit to his sobriety, and he was one of the reasons I never drank again after 1997.

Galatians 6:2 says, "Carry each other's burdens, and in this way, you will fulfill the law of Christ." That kind of accountability is what God calls us to offer to one another.

Not every relationship, business or personal, had a happy ending. I had a partner named Tony who struggled deeply with addiction. He and I had started a business together, an outdoor motocross team and a supercross team. We had several riders with a privateer sponsorship from Kawasaki for parts, frames, etc., Marathon Motor Coaches for the trailer, and Volvo for the tractor cab. We spent the year attending all the outdoor motocross races on the US East Coast and, as well as the East Coast Supercross series. I was excited, and it was fun being at the races.

We were on our way to having a Craftsman Truck race team with a shop in Mooresville, NC. The shop had been selected, and the sponsors were falling into line. We were going to be one of the first teams to have a Toyota sponsorship.

Just before finalizing everything and getting ready for the first season, the wheels fell off, so to speak, with my personal and professional relationship with Tony. This guy could have one drink, and he literally turned into Dr. Jekyll and Mr. Hyde. You wouldn't even believe the transformation from one drink. He had five, six, seven DUIs and jail time in his past. He couldn't escape it, and it destroyed our friendship and business. Some wounds never fully heal. I tried to help him, but he just didn't want help, and we ultimately parted ways.

I also had a lifelong friend, Dave, who I've been friends with since I was 12 years old. He battled his own demons, and our relationship went through periods, partnership, betrayal, years of silence, then reconnection. Dave and I were business partners before my wife and I met, and Dave and I had a falling out; I took it very personally. I can remember having conversations with my Uncle Jack about what I felt was a betrayal. Dave and I didn't talk for some time, but I never really ever turned my back on him; after all, it would be the last time we had a falling out.

131

At that point, I learned a lesson about not drawing lines in the sand. I'm a huge proponent of it. In the Marine Corps, you never know when you need to cross the bridge again. My uncle Jack and his law partner, Larry, hadn't spoken for 20-something years. I tried for five years to help foster that relationship and successfully got them to talk. They became good friends again before it was too late. As for Dave, our paths crossed many more times; some of those times, he was working with me or for me. Most of those times ended with some sort of parting.

You will always have arguments and disagreements with friends and family, but you must use your faith and sometimes bridge the gap, swallowing your pride to keep that relationship intact. Most of the time, you will find it was petty or humorous in later years. The adage of "time heals all" is so true, at least in my 50 years of experience.

Matthew 18:21-22 says, "Then Peter came to Jesus and asked, 'Lord, how many times shall I forgive my brother or sister who sins against me? Up to seven times?' Jesus answered, 'I tell you, not seven times, but seventy-seven times.'" This verse is a great core principle in relationships.

With Dave, I drew that line in the sand again, and we didn't talk for three years. Then, one day, just out of the blue, I had a feeling that I should just pick up the phone and call him. I know that was God right there telling me to check on him. I hadn't talked to him in three years, and when I called, I found out his wife had been living with her son, and he was living in the back of a semi-trailer, trying to make a tiny home out of it, just no place to live, struggling.

It was meant to be that I called him on that day because I had a piece of property with a vacant house on it. I said, "You can live in there, rent-free. Get back on your feet." He lived there for about two years. Then, when I sold that property, God's timing was perfect, I had another house in downtown Orlando that was vacant.

This wasn't a coincidence. When something pops up and you think, "I can't believe it", like when you can't pay your electric bill and the next day you get a check in the mail or a job offer, that's God at work. When you're trying to help a friend who's living rent-free in a house you have to sell, and suddenly you have another vacant house available, that's divine timing. Those aren't accidents. You just have to know that's God working in your life. There's no other explanation, and you don't need one. You have that faith and trust it.

Isaiah 55:8-9 says, "For my thoughts are not your thoughts, neither are your ways my ways,' declares the Lord. 'As the heavens are higher than the earth, so are my ways higher than your ways and my thoughts than your thoughts." Sometimes, we can't understand God's timing, but we can trust His perfect plan.

Another friend who had personal struggles was Carl. He spiraled publicly and dangerously into addiction early in 2000. He just hit rock bottom, and the drinking nearly destroyed him and his family. He decided enough was enough and literally left for a treatment facility in another state for almost a year.

I didn't know how to help, but I did what I could: I texted him encouragement randomly when I felt God pushing me to do so. Some of the things I was texting him just seemed to be so divine, straight from God, things I wouldn't usually say in a text. I felt these things flowing through me: "You can do it, one day at a time. God loves you, and we love you." It was almost an out-of-body experience.

I remember getting replies back like, "Hey, bro, thank you. It's the right time to get this. I really needed that." I knew I was sending those because God wanted me to send them at that particular time. They always seemed to land at the right moment. He later told me they helped keep him going.

1 Thessalonians 5:11 says, "Therefore encourage one another and build each other up, just as in fact you are doing." Ultimately, Carl came back successful and changed his life. He really soaked up God, and that faith continued to grow. His family is better for it, and he leads an amazing life of great faith today.

Then there was Duncan. My fishing buddy. My friend. We met in the early 1980s when we were both attending Northland Church. He married a great girl who was friends with my wife, and he had two beautiful children. We became close, fishing professional tournaments together in the SKA Southern King Fishing Association, OBoy Oberta Red Fish Cup series, and one in particular, a series called Fisher of Men, and we had deep, spiritual fellowship.

But Duncan battled alcohol and depression for years. When I started PremiereTrade, I brought him on as a platform speaker, and I said, "You can't drink. If you drink, I have to let you go." He quit for two years, and that was good for him and his family. Then he started drinking again, and it was really rough from then on out.

He couldn't escape his addiction. He was Baker Acted multiple times, found on the side of the road with a gun in his hand, and reached out constantly for help. I tried to be there for him. We spent hours on the phone daily. I sent prayers, encouragement, love. I would text him these profound messages that I felt were coming straight from God, and he'd say, "Perfect time. Thank you. I needed this."

Then he'd text me back: "I can't do it. I can't go any longer. I don't know what to do." I would press and press: "God loves you. We all love you. You've got to do it for you and your family. God wants you to be great."

I prayed to God to show me how to help him: "Give me the strength to say the right things. Don't let me say the wrong thing." But one day, after a particularly difficult hour-and-a-half conversation that was probably one of the hardest I'd ever had with him as far as despair goes, he took his own life the next day.

That wounded me deeply and emotionally. I questioned God. Did I do enough? Did I say the wrong thing? Why? I just rarely have ever said, "God, why?" But I was like, "Why? Why did this happen? Did I not do enough? Did I not say enough?" It just weighed on me. It was a horrible feeling. I must add that a good friend of mine, whom Duncan introduced me to, was right there every step of the way with Duncan as well. Chad and I, along with our families, are really close to this day.

I realized that my experience with Duncan helped me help Carl. When Carl was struggling, I delivered those words of encouragement with more faith and vigor than you could ever imagine, knowing that they made a difference. I wasn't going to let the same thing happen. God doesn't waste anything. He uses our pain, our losses, and our scars to help someone else.

This chapter is about that truth. God will use you to reach people. If you feel that nudge to call someone, do it. If you think of someone randomly, it's not random, reach out to them. Don't wait. Text them. Email them. Speak life. It might be the message they need most. And you might be the only one who can deliver it at that moment.

This chapter is also a reminder that God uses relationships to build and test our faith. And sometimes, the people we're meant to help are the ones whose stories teach us the most.

Every relationship God brings into our lives, whether for a period of joy or a period of pain, is designed to sharpen us and prepare us for His purposes.

# CHAPTER 10

# Faith-Based Entrepreneurship

*Building Businesses with God at the Center*

In the last chapter, we discussed divine intervention, where God puts people in our lives at the right time for the right reasons, or at least for His purposes. I want to explore how faith can work with entrepreneurship and business. Some of the most important lessons I've learned have come from building new businesses, as well as from businesses that didn't work out and those that were struggling. All of these experiences have helped me grow in my faith and better understand my Christian journey.

I've been called a serial entrepreneur, and whether that's a curse or a gift is left to be determined. As someone who has started multiple businesses over the years, the biggest thing I've learned is that I get bored once something is almost finished, stabilized, and generating revenue. There's no challenge, so I'm always looking for the next one. And you know what? It takes tremendous faith to accomplish that. One of the reasons I love the development side of real estate is that every deal is different, every community and project is different, and you never have the same thing twice, from the time you locate and contract the property to the time houses and town centers are built, every time it is different.

Before I founded PremiereTrade, I worked in business development for a company where I developed an entire business model centered on trading currencies. I had worked my way up to being a lecturer, traveling around the country, and making more money a year than ever before. It was the most I had ever made working for someone else. But things weren't working out, both in the promises made to me and what I wanted to do versus what I felt I should do. I essentially just left and started my own business.

It was very scary at that point. Starting your own business always is. However, within six months, I found more opportunities and continued to grow, and that business eventually reached 250 employees and was making tremendous revenue. Then came the Great Financial Crisis of 2007-2008. Through various over-regulation and economic factors, the business went from 250 employees to zero overnight. Here, I had this business worth tens of millions, and overnight, it went to zero.

I had to start over from scratch, and that's happened to me multiple times in my life. In my early years, when I was starting out or had a new family, those were tougher times, and taking risks was harder. But I've always believed and had these dreams that this is what I was meant to do; this is what I'm supposed to do. And I've always followed that dream.

Proverbs 16:9 says, "In their hearts, humans plan their course, but the Lord establishes their steps." I've learned that no matter how well we plan, God is ultimately directing our path.

I can remember a specific example of this from the early 2000s with PremiereTrade. We had started with just an alert service called Premier FX Alerts, and we were taking the next step to create PremiereTrade. Even more importantly, we were developing what we called DATS, Direct Access Trading System.

We brought on smart people, including some guys who used to work for the Defense Intelligence Agency. They understood compression technology because we were aggregating financial data directly from the exchanges, the New York Stock Exchange, AMEX, the CBOE, and others.

To take this to the next level, we needed to bring on more engineers who were specifically familiar with the space we were in. My faith was strong at that point, and I'd be praying a lot: "God, give me some direction. What should we be doing? Send me some opportunities that I'll recognize and that will help me take my business to the next level." I was starting to feel the pressure and responsibility of all the people and their families who were employed by PremiereTrade.

We were in a building in Altamonte Springs, Florida, and there was a company on the third floor called Globe Net Crossing. There were around 15 people up there. They were working with cutting-edge technology related to ECNs, Electronic Communication Networks, like Island

and Archipelago, disseminating information and connecting buyers and sellers directly in the marketplace. It was exactly the kind of technology we wanted to be part of.

Then Globe Net Crossing was bought out by Archipelago, and they essentially gave everybody pink slips and closed the office. I remember thinking, "This is an opportunity. These people just lost their jobs. They need work. They're super smart, and they've been building exactly the technology we need."

As they walked out the door, literally leaving their office and coming out of the elevators, I was standing there, talking to them and offering them jobs. I ended up hiring a couple of those software engineers right on the spot. They came in and helped us accomplish exactly what we needed with PremiereTrade, creating the direct-access trading technology that's still in use with PremiereTrade today.

Here's something we really needed. We were somewhat stuck and didn't know how to get to the next level. All of a sudden, this opportunity arose. People were losing their jobs, and we were able to bring them on, give them employment, and ultimately create something that benefited everyone. That's how God works in business when you're seeking His direction and staying open to the opportunities He provides.

One thing I learned through faith early on is the power of writing down your dreams and goals. When I was around 15 or 16 years old, someone challenged me to write down my long-term goals, short-term goals, and dreams. If I had all the money and time in the world, what would I want? I found that list some 15 years later, and it was interesting to note what was on there: I wanted to own a house worth $250,000, I wanted to be a fighter pilot, I wanted to have a million dollars, all the things you'd dream about as a young kid.

What I discovered is that when you write that stuff down, it begins to take root in your subconscious. Suddenly, your dreams start to become your long-term goals, your long-term goals start to become your short-term goals, and you accomplish your short-term goals. That's something you really need to challenge yourself to do every year or so, write those down and continue to update them.

Long story short, I was able to meet most of my dreams, including flying in an F-18 with a friend of mine who was a Marine aviator for the Blue Angels in 2006. I spent about an hour and a half going Mach 2, about 1,800 miles an hour, essentially with my hair on fire. It came from all the relationships I built in the military.

But here's what I've learned: putting a monetary or material value on your dreams creates a void in your life, one that lacks faith and personal connection to God. Those things don't really matter in the end.

Ecclesiastes 5:10 says, "Whoever loves money never has enough; whoever loves wealth is never satisfied with their income. This, too, is meaningless." I've experienced this firsthand; I made my first million by 30 and lost it by 31; I always joked in my presentations that it was a good year! You see, it's easy to make money, much harder to keep it.

I was doing some personal Bible study and finished reading Proverbs, then moved straight into Ecclesiastes. My son James and I were discussing both books and during our conversation, I learned that Solomon wrote Ecclesiastes. But here's what got me - Ecclesiastes isn't just wisdom; its wisdom earned through experience, shared so others can live with purpose instead of chasing empty things.

I was thinking how ironic it is that this discussion comes up while I'm writing a book on God's grace and my experiences. That's God working in my life right there.

This is a book written by someone older, looking back and saying: "Here's what I've learned from my years of experience. Don't make the same mistakes I did." The timing and irony of studying a book about wisdom through experience while writing your book about wisdom through experience is a perfect example of divine timing.

So, what do you do when your business is struggling or failing? What do you do in catastrophic situations where the economy falls apart and you go from 250 employees to none? We've talked about this in the book before: You have to get up the next morning, pull up your bootstraps, and go to work. Figure out what you're going to do and start doing it. Start making things happen. You have to do it!

You have to have faith and believe that there's a reason behind all this, and whatever it is, it's going to make you a better, stronger person as long as you maintain that faith. It will show itself and reveal itself at some point, and the light bulb will go off: "I get it. I see it."

I used to think, "Why me? Why can't I get this over the hump? Why can't I make more money?" But hindsight being 20/20, I look back and say, "Oh, now I know why I learned that lesson. Now I know why I have that experience", because somebody's going to come to me struggling and need some help and assistance.

James 1:2-4 says, "Consider it pure joy, my brothers and sisters, whenever you face trials of many kinds because you know that the testing of your faith produces perseverance. Let perseverance finish its work so that you may be mature and complete, not lacking anything." I've learned this the hard way through all the ups and downs of my business.

When people come up to me and they're struggling, their business may not be performing, they may be heavily leveraged, or they've got all their money sunk into something, we have a conversation. It all starts with: "How's your faith? How's your relationship with God?" Because you can go out there and try to do all these things you want to do, but if those aren't right, your business isn't going to be right.

So, I ask them, 'Are you doing something good?' Is it making people's lives better around you? What is your balance between family, spiritual life, and business? Where is that balance? It's hard when you're building a business to focus on what is right and what's wrong.

I always say that just because you're struggling right now doesn't mean you're failing. All that means is that you're missing something. There's something you need to focus on to make a difference. And remember just do it. Make a phone call. Call ten people. Ask them for input or insight, people you know, people you've met. You'll find that your business starts moving. Your faith starts growing, and you become more balanced.

Just because it's failing doesn't mean it can't succeed. It just means you need to put in the effort to stop the problems. You need to recognize what that is and know that God has you where you need to be. That gives you peace of mind, whether you're involved in a big business or a small business, even owning a restaurant that may be struggling.

You also need to understand that it may not be the right fit for you. You may have gotten into it at the wrong time. It may not be the right thing to do. Maybe you need to take the lessons you've learned, and God wants you to apply those somewhere else in life. You may need to move on. Those are hard things. Those are things you should be praying about.

Matthew 6:33 says, "But seek first his kingdom and his righteousness, and all these things will be given to you as well." When you put God first in your business decisions, everything else falls into place.

Speaking of prayer, I heard something in a recent sermon that got me thinking. Are your prayers making God better in your life? Are they making someone else better? Are you just asking for yourself? It's okay to pray for your own needs, but you really need to examine your heart.

I always wonder: Am I praying right? Am I saying the right things? But that comes from your relationship with God. When you're reading the Word and have Scripture in your life, the more you're involved in church, the more you're around other believers, the more you understand, the closer you get to God, and the easier it becomes to answer those questions.

This will lift up your life, lift up your business, lift up your family. It'll make you a better person. It'll help you give back. Everything you do should involve giving back to others. We're going to talk about that more in the next chapter, but I tell people all the time: if you've been blessed to make a lot of money, then you should continue to do that. You shouldn't just say, "I made all the money I need to make, and I'm done."

You should look at how that blessing God gave you can help others.

There have been many times when I've made a ton of money and lost a ton of money, learned from those experiences, and the next time out was even better. But along the way, I continue to give back. Service to others brings balance and makes your life complete, and doing all of that for God's will is the way to earn His favor.

In this chapter, I also want to discuss the role of mentors. I've written about this in other books, and I think everybody in life has to have a mentor, whether that's your pastor, your best friend, your parents, your father, your grandfather, your neighbor, or somebody who's already been successful that you have access to. Everybody needs a mentor to get ahead.

It's especially valuable to find a Christian mentor with a deeply rooted value system rooted in their faith. That can certainly help you. For instance, Buddy, whom I've discussed in this book, was one of those mentors. I've had many mentors in my life across many different subjects, specifically faith-based, spiritual, and business crossed over with faith-based.

One thing you'll discover is that a lot of mentors say the same thing. That's why you see all these people online selling coaching and life coaching programs. In the end, they say the same thing, and whether you pay for it or not is up to you. But really, what you're looking for is that mentor you connect with, someone who, when they say something to you, means something. A light bulb goes off, and you feel it: "I can go do this. I can take that advice. I see myself making that happen."

Even though your dad, mom, or someone else may have already told you the same thing and you didn't listen, that's okay as long as you can find a mentor and act on their guidance. A lot of times that could be your pastor, depending on what kind of church you go to. Some pastors possess the entrepreneurial gene and may offer valuable advice for you. In the end, they're going to be able to help you come back to God and incorporate Him into what you're doing.

I often hear people say, "I want to own my own business." It could be young people, and it could be older folks looking for a change. But here's the thing - owning your own business is a different animal altogether.

When you own your own business, you are your boss. You don't have anybody to look up to except for God. And you'll be asking for guidance and wisdom in your prayers - trust me, you'll need it.

You must be prepared to have immense faith, especially during those early startup years. It typically takes five to seven years to create a company with real value - something that can be potentially sold, or that becomes truly sustainable. Until then, you're working your job until you figure it out.

And it's not about how much money you make. It's really about the journey. Because owning your own business isn't easy, you'll be working 70, 80, or maybe 100 hours a week. I remember in many of the businesses I've started -

they don't all work out, for whatever reasons - you have to be prepared to accept that risk. You could go from hero to zero pretty quickly.

Maybe your business fails, or it's not viable anymore. Maybe you didn't adjust fast enough. Whatever the reason, you've got to be able to pick yourself up and start over. And you've got to do it quickly.

In the beginning, you're doing everything. The books, the accounting, the banking. Accounts payable and receivable. You're buying inventory, taking sales calls, making appointments - all of it. As the business grows, maybe you can take some of that off your plate. But that's the reality.

It's not really about making all the money. It's about the journey you go through. It's about the families you help and the employees you support. It's about the network you build and the people you meet along the way. Those testimonials from customers and employees - that's what inspires you and keeps you motivated to keep moving forward.

Proverbs 21:5 says, "The plans of the diligent lead to profit as surely as haste leads to poverty." I've learned this the hard way - both sides of it. When I've been diligent, patient, and careful with my planning, businesses have succeeded. When I've rushed into things or cut corners, well, that's when I've gone from hero to zero pretty quickly. God honors diligent work, but He also teaches us through our failures when we try to take shortcuts.

When you put God at the center of your business decisions, when you seek His will first, when you use your success to bless others, that's when you discover what real entrepreneurship is all about.

In the next chapter, we'll dive deeper into giving back and how service to others becomes the foundation for a life of purpose and fulfillment.

# CHAPTER 11

## Called To Serve

*Time, Talent, and Treasure*

We just finished talking about faith-based entrepreneurship, and now I want to dive into something that's become one of the most important parts of my life, giving back. I'm blessed to be able to do it, and honestly, service has become essential to how I live out my faith in real, practical ways.

I currently sit on several boards and foundations. Through all this work, I've learned something pretty simple: giving back comes in one of three forms, time, talent, or treasure. Not everybody can write big checks. Not everybody has hours to volunteer. And we all have different skills to offer. But everyone has something they can contribute somehow. For me, it's always been about trying to give back in whatever way I can.

One of my earliest memories of service, was when I was seven or eight. I was in Cub Scouts, and my mom was one of the leaders. We'd meet in this little volunteer fire department in Mount Snow, Vermont. Just a small firehouse with a room above where the fire truck was parked. It had these big sirens on top of the building.

When those sirens went off, volunteer firemen would drop whatever they were doing and come running to help put out fires. No cell phones, no pagers, just those loud sirens. Even as a little kid, I could see people serving their community. That's probably one of my first memories of what giving back looked like.

I also remember helping at my dad's hotel when I was maybe five or six. We'd get these bus tours full of retirees who came to see the fall leaves. We called them "leaf peepers." I'd help carry their luggage to their rooms. Even then, something in me wanted to help others. The occasional quarter I got was nice, but I think I just liked being useful.

Matthew 25:40 says, "The King will reply, 'Truly I tell you, whatever you did for one of the least of these brothers and sisters of mine, you did for me.'" Looking back, I can see God was already shaping my heart for service, even as a child.

Fast-forward to Hurricane Katrina. That's when I really felt this huge need to give back in a bigger way. At the time, we were selling PremiereTrade software for $3,000 all around the world. I kept thinking, "I've got to find some way to help these people."

So, we launched this campaign to our entire database: "Here's your opportunity. If you've been thinking about buying the software, buy it today, and we'll donate 100% of the proceeds to Hurricane Katrina relief." We raised $350,000 and donated every penny to the Red Cross. That felt incredible. It was that whole time, talent, and treasure thing in action.

I think by God's grace, I've been able to grow in my ability to give back while keeping everything balanced with business and family. The next big step was ESGR, Employer Support of the Guard and Reserve. We talked about that in earlier chapters. I started volunteering in 2008 and kept going through 2020. In 2015, the Secretary of Defense appointed me to serve as state chairman here in Florida, two three-year tours.

Through ESGR, I was putting in 1,000 to 1,500 hours a year serving our country and community. Looking back, joining the Marine Corps was another way to serve. ESGR, let me continue that calling. Even now, I'm still the boss lift coordinator, and I'd love to do more as I get older.

I was definitely one of the younger people in ESGR. It's mostly populated by retirees, people who served their whole lives in the military and want to keep giving back. Or their spouses. Or people who never got the chance to serve but want to serve their country somehow. It's a great mission that's really close to my heart.

At one point, I actually applied to be the national chair. That's a huge position; it carries a three-star general protocol. A good friend of mine, who was the Secretary of the VA, wrote me a letter of reference. This guy was a West Point graduate and ran Procter & Gamble for 15 years. I made it to the final two.

I came in second. The person who got it was the former director of the Defense Intelligence Agency with a resume about 30 pages long. Here I was, a younger guy with no college degree, just a sense of service, and I got that close. Maybe I'll have another shot when I'm older and more seasoned. We'll see what God has planned.

Acts 20:35 reminds us, "In everything I did, I showed you that by this kind of hard work, we must help the weak, remembering the words the Lord Jesus himself said: 'It is more blessed to give than to receive.'" That's become a guiding principle in all my service work.

Now, let me tell you about something I'm really proud of, what we're doing for law enforcement. We've set up several sheriff's foundations, and this vision came from Don Prewitt, who I've known forever. He calls me his son. His actual son, Scott, is the VP of my development company. Scott and I have worked together for over 35 years. He gets this call to service, he's been a deacon at his church for 20 years, there every Sunday.

I was a founding member of the Seminole County Sheriff's Foundation, I'm president now. The Orange County Sheriff's Foundation was the first one we set up. I sit on the board, as well as the Orlando Police Foundation. I founded and was the first president of the Osceola County Sheriff's Foundation. I also set up St. Johns County and Citrus County, I'm president of both of those, too.

This is our way of giving back to the people who serve our communities. I call it "911 financial assistance." When officers or deputies need help, there's usually support available, but sometimes it takes forever to get to them. We pride ourselves on turning requests around in 24 hours and getting money in people's hands when they really need it.

These foundations started for families who lost someone in the line of duty. Thankfully, that doesn't happen as much anymore because of better training and support. What we're mostly dealing with now are medical issues, cancer treatments, huge insurance deductibles, someone's been sick and used up all their time off. We step in and solve those immediate financial problems.

We've raised millions and given back millions to this cause. We help everyone at the sheriff's offices and police departments, sworn officers, civilian employees, and their families. It's a legacy that will last forever.

A few years ago, I received a call about a young woman at the UCF Police Department. She'd been in a car crash. Physically, she was okay, but financially it was a disaster. Her insurance wasn't enough to cover the damage. She couldn't afford to have her car properly fixed. She was borrowing another officer's car to get to work.

Three days before Christmas, Diane Dello Russo brought this situation to my attention. Diane has been a huge supporter of law enforcement; she's someone who truly understands the importance of giving back and making things happen. She made a significant donation herself and also established a connection with the car dealer, which proved to be the key to everything. I just made sure things moved quickly and got the other foundations involved.

Christmas Eve, I met her and her 11-year-old daughter at the dealership. We presented them with an almost brand-new car, only 10,000 miles and a five-year warranty. Both of them were crying. It was one of those moments that reminds you why we do this work, being able to step in fast when someone who serves our community is struggling.

That's exactly what I mean by "911 financial assistance." Other support systems might take weeks or months. We can get money in someone's hands in 24 hours. I saw God working a miracle right there. I was just part of His plan for this officer and her daughter. The tears of relief on their faces, she knew this was God giving her favor. I'm sure that Christmas was extra emotional for them.

2 Corinthians 9:7 says, "Each of you should give what you have decided in your heart to give, not reluctantly or under compulsion, for God loves a cheerful giver." That's our approach with these foundations; we give cheerfully because we know we're serving God's people.

My friend Eric works with one of the national builders. Since we do a lot of work with national builders, Eric came up with this great idea called the Hero Home. We're on our fourth one now. Either a developer or builder donates a lot, or sometimes the foundation buys one, and we build a house on it.

Eric goes to all his vendors and says, "Here's what we're doing. Want to support it?" We get 100% buy-in. Everyone donates their time, talent, and treasure. They donate the drywall, AC, electrical, pool, pavers, driveway, fencing, everything that goes into building a house, including furniture. Everything is donated, so we owe nothing.

Then we sell these houses, the first one sold for $260,000. We just sold one for $760,000. One hundred percent of those proceeds go back to the foundations. It's helping us build endowments, something that'll be there for generations.

We host an annual Blue Line Gala, which attracts approximately 1,000 people and raises around $500,000. One of the Foundations just did a fishing tournament and raised $75,000. A golf tournament is held every year, resulting in another $80,000. Each foundation has its ways of raising money, plus we do big projects like the Hero Homes, where multiple foundations work together.

It's such a great feeling. It's such a worthy cause. These foundations are practical ways to live out God's command to serve others, especially those who protect our communities.

I also sit on the AdventHealth Heart, Lung, and Vascular Institute Foundation. AdventHealth is a great

Christian organization. We raise millions to support the community and people in need.

When I first joined the AdventHealth board, they wanted me to really understand what the foundation supports. They offered me this incredible experience, scrubbing in for open heart surgery with Dr. Palmer at AdventHealth South in Orlando. I was nervous, not sure what I'd see or if I could handle it. But I said yes, knowing it would make me a better board member.

I showed up and met the surgical team. They brought me to the cardiac unit; I scrubbed in, put on scrubs, and went to the operating room. When I walked in, honestly, it was overwhelming. I looked around and tried to embrace the moment. Here I am, this tough Marine, and I found myself praying, "Lord, don't let me pass out. Let me stay focused and listen."

It's very private. You don't come in until after the patient's prepped, so you don't really know who it is. But you're right there, standing on a stool at the surgical table, looking down at what the surgeon's doing. It was really overwhelming, knowing my father had several open-heart surgeries and my grandfather died from a heart attack. Deeply emotional for me, knowing this is somebody's father, husband, brother, friend, and he's in the hands of these surgeons.

One of the big moments is when they put the patient on the bypass pump. All the blood is now being pumped through a mechanical device. The sights and smells are indescribable. But what I can describe is this room, it's like an orchestra, and the surgeon is conducting. One surgeon, one assisting surgeon, and probably seven or eight surgical techs. Machines everywhere. Everything is quiet, organized, and focused.

Many of these surgical techs are young, right out of school. They could graduate from high school, attend surgical tech school for two years, and then work alongside surgeons in surgeries. Some are harvesting veins from the legs for the heart grafts.

I've always respected surgical techs. I have a really good friend from high school, Jerry, who works at Tampa General Hospital. He got me a job there years ago. We were roommates a couple of different times. It's just admirable work. He's been there for over 30 years now. He's on the organ transplant team now. He gets on private planes or helicopters with surgical teams to harvest organs from donors and bring them back for transplant surgery.

He started just like those young people I saw in that room. Prepping patients, getting them to surgery, assisting surgeons, and harvesting veins. It's really admirable work. Standing there had a double meaning for me. I got to see firsthand what my friend Jerry had been doing all these years. And these surgeons, they're like angels, in my opinion. They have patients' lives in their hands. They're the difference between someone living or not. Everything that happens in that room, everything that happens to that patient, it's God's plan. God planned to have those surgeons there that day to save this person's life and let them go back to their families.

After the operating room, we went to recovery and saw the whole process, recovery to ICU, then to regular rooms with families, complete circle. We even went through the pediatric heart center. That was overwhelming, too. But knowing we have this amazing Christian hospital helping all these people, that's why I wanted to stay on that board.

Galatians 6:9-10 says, "Let us not become weary in doing good, for at the proper time we will reap a harvest if we do not give up. Therefore, as we have the opportunity, let us do good to all people, especially to those who belong to the family of believers." That captures perfectly why we continue to do this work, serving others is serving God.

Speaking of using your network to serve others, I want to tell you about something that happened during COVID that really showed me how God uses the connections He helps you build over the years.

In 2019 and 2020, at the height of COVID, Jerry Smith and I started talking a lot. Jerrys in this book - he goes way back to the DNA Pulse days. He was actually one of our clients. He was the CEO of a sleep apnea company in Tampa, and we did social media marketing for him.

Through that work, Jerry and I struck up a relationship. We ended up doing some pro bono work for a nonprofit he was involved with - the Children's Leukemia Foundation. He was on their board, and we did Facebook marketing for them for free. The crazy thing is that the work we set up created this legacy that just kept raising money automatically for about 10 years. They didn't have to do anything - it just kept working. That felt good.

But during COVID, with not much else going on, Jerry and I would talk on the phone constantly. I had connections within the military, the Florida National Guard, and the state government, including the Executive Director of Emergency Management.

There came a time when Florida was struggling to obtain personal protective equipment (PPE). Everybody was affected, including hospitals, due to supply chain issues and our reliance on other countries for everything. We felt compelled to help.

I'd spoken to people I knew in the National Guard who were looking for anybody who could source this stuff. Jerry and I dug into it a bit. We really learned a lot about that business, and within a short period, we became one of the go-to people that officials would call to talk about what was happening in the industry.

Let me tell you - it was almost like a book in itself. All the craziness, all the brokerages, and middlemen, all the fraud. It was unbelievable, like a reality TV show, but with people's lives at stake.

Jerry and I really dug in. We have created a vast network worldwide, with contacts in China and throughout the rest of the world. In the end, we were able to source some PPE. However, it was a daunting and never-ending task that seemed almost impossible.

We had people traveling all over the country. People in other countries are trying to put their eyes on actual equipment. We were talking to huge multinational companies. Most of it led nowhere, but we kept trying because we felt like this was what we were supposed to be doing.

Isaiah 6:8 says, "Then I heard the voice of the Lord saying, 'Whom shall I send? And who will go for us?' And I said, 'Here am I. Send me! '" That's exactly how I felt during that time. When you see a need, and you have the ability to help - even if you're not sure you can actually solve it - you step up. You use whatever network and resources God has given you.

Jerry and I spent countless hours on the phone during that period. It really built a lasting relationship that's continued into his work with me at DIX Developments now. He assists with capital market structures and communication efforts for our various projects, including both municipal and neighborhood communications.

Sometimes, God puts you in situations not because you're going to save the day but because He's building relationships and preparing you for what comes next. That whole COVID experience strengthened my friendship with Jerry and positioned us both for the work we're doing together today.

Galatians 6:9-10 says, "Let us not become weary in doing good, for at the proper time we will reap a harvest if we do not give up. Therefore, as we have the opportunity, let us do good to all people, especially to those who belong to the family of believers." That perfectly captures why we continue to do this work, serving others is serving God.

What I've learned through all these years of service is that giving back isn't just about writing checks; it's about making a meaningful impact. It's about using whatever God's given you, time, talents, resources, to make a difference in people's lives. Whether it's a six-year-old carrying luggage, a businessman donating hurricane relief funds, or foundations supporting first responders, it all comes down to the same thing: we're called to serve.

This balance of service has taught me that real success isn't measured by what you pile up but by what you give away and how you use your blessings to bless others. Every foundation I'm on, every hour I volunteer, every dollar we raise, it's all part of living out my faith in practical ways.

I wouldn't be doing this chapter justice if I didn't mention my wife, Deb. Twenty-six years of marriage, and she's been instrumental in my ability to give back and serve on these boards. Her selfless support makes all of this possible. She gets me. She understands my need to serve and give back. She has her causes she believes in and supports, too.

Speaking of family, Deb and I taught our kids about the importance of service from a young age. When James was about eight, and Jacki was maybe 4, Deb helped them set up a lemonade stand on the curb in front of our house. The kids collected all the proceeds and put them in a ziplock bag. Then, as a family, we all drove down to a women's shelter in Orlando and donated the money.

I'll never forget how proud James and Jacki were. They knew they were helping others, and you could see it meant something to them. That lesson stuck.

Their service continues in multiple ways around our community today. All three of them, Deb, James, and Jacki, support ESGR and the sheriff's foundations. I'm very proud of my whole family for understanding that serving others is just part of who we are.

In the next chapter, we'll explore how this heart for service extends into other areas and how God keeps opening doors for greater impact.

# CHAPTER 12

# Living The Legacy

## *Mentoring the Next Generation*

As When I look back on my journey, through successes and setbacks, all the ups and downs, what keeps coming back to me is this: faith isn't just something you talk about; it's something you live. It's something you live. Real faith has legs. It moves. It shows up in what you do.

I think you have to live your faith. Not everyone's called to be a pastor, but we're all called to minister somehow, through business, through service, through friendship, through just not giving up. Over the years, I've realized that living out your faith doesn't require a pulpit. Sometimes, it just takes a phone call, a conversation, or doing the right thing when nobody's watching.

I've had years where everything was clicking, business was good, family was healthy. But I've had more years where things got tough. There was a time when I had 250 employees, and overnight, because of government overreach and the financial crisis, I had to let them all go. That wasn't just a financial hit. It was personal. I carried the weight of those families, their mortgages, their kids' needs, their futures.

That kind of blow makes you question everything. Your decisions, your ability, even your faith. But that's when faith reminds you: you may have lost your footing, but God hasn't lost you.

In moments like that, I'd turn to prayer, then to action. I'd get up the next day, even when it felt impossible, and make the calls. Start over. And each time I did, something would shift. A door would open. A connection would come through. I learned that faith isn't about waiting for the storm to pass. It's about walking through it, knowing that God has something in mind for you.

Luke 12:11-12 says, "When you are brought before synagogues, rulers and authorities, do not worry about how you will defend yourselves or what you will say, for the Holy Spirit will teach you at that time what you should say." I've experienced this countless times, in business meetings, conversations with struggling friends, and especially mentoring young people. God gives you the words when you need them.

That's guided me in mentoring others. I've had business owners, young entrepreneurs, and even pastors come to me asking, "How do I build something that lasts? How do I market my brand? What do I do when my business is failing or struggling?" And here's what I've figured out over the years - the first question I ask myself is: 'What does my relationship with God look like right now?' And that's the same question they should be asking themselves. Because if that's not aligned, nothing else will be. When God's at the center, the rest can fall into place, even if it takes time.

Faith in action also means obedience, even when it's uncomfortable. Picking up the phone to call someone you've fallen out with. Giving generously when you're not sure what's around the corner. Doing the right thing when nobody's there to applaud.

I've seen this play out in big and small ways. Setting up sheriff's foundations, writing checks for medical bills, and helping put a Hero Home project together. I try to respond when I feel God nudge me. When you feel that pull, that stirring, "Call him," "Help her," "Speak up", you can't ignore it.

During this next phase of my growth in faith, I feel more inclined to share my testimony with those who feel or say they're missing something in their life. My reply is simple: you're missing God in your life. My pastor recently said, "You can be bold in a whisper." That hit me. You can share your faith boldly without being pushy about it. God's words will be there when you need them. You can whisper His truth into someone's life and watch it transform them.

Philippians 1:27 says, "Whatever happens, conduct yourselves in a manner worthy of the gospel of Christ." That's become my approach to mentoring, not just talking to young people about what to do but showing them through how I live.

I remember when Larry asked if I'd spend a week with his daughter, who was at Florida State. He wanted me to show her what I do in business on a daily basis. I said sure. She showed up Monday at 9 AM, and I had the whole week planned to show her real estate development.

We'd start each day talking about the news, then discussing what we were going to do. That week, we went to meetings with county officials in two different counties to discuss projects. She got to see firsthand what we did and heard my phone conversations while driving. By the end of the week, she felt she'd learned a lot. Her father kept telling me how much she was getting out of it.

The next young person showed up soon after. My partner, Alexis, called and asked if his son, who had recently graduated from college, could shadow me to learn about our business. At first, I thought, "Okay, Alexis Jr. is coming to keep an eye on me," though I knew that wasn't really the case. I said sure. "How long are you thinking?" After doing a week with Larry's daughter, I expected something similar. Alexis said, "I'm thinking like five months." Five months? Reeeeally?

Well, Alexis Jr. moved to Lake Mary, got an apartment, and started working with my son and me. As the months went by, I realized his father wanted him to see something outside Miami, learn about discipline, dedication, and some Marine Corps values: honor, courage, and commitment. That's what I taught him. Leadership skills, the business, and more. His five months became two years. He stayed through his master's degree, then moved home and went to work for KPMG. A year later, he was working for his dad on our business ventures. He's one of the people I'm most proud of mentoring, and I know I will go on to great things.

2 Timothy 2:2 reminds us, "And the things you have heard me say in the presence of many witnesses entrust to reliable people who will also be qualified to teach others." That's become the foundation of how I approach mentoring, passing on not just business knowledge but life principles that can be shared with the next generation.

I look at these as opportunities to help mold future leaders and give them a foundation they don't get in school. It's not really about learning my business, it's about life lessons and sharing experiences some would consider mistakes. I try to teach them to think outside the box and never give up. I'd pray before these periods of instruction, asking God to give me strength to be a good teacher and make a lasting difference.

It's not just the parent with faith, it's me, with my faith in Jesus Christ, knowing I'm where I'm supposed to be, with whom I'm supposed to be, saying what I'm supposed to say. It's truly an honor to be asked to share your experiences with a young, impressionable person, and that comes with great responsibility that I do not take lightly.

I have a library at my office with hundreds of books, many of which are religious, some are about entrepreneurship or business, some are about trading, some are fiction, and others cover a range of technical topics and various subjects. I collected these over the years. I received a large collection when my father passed away, and upon reviewing it, I noticed he'd highlighted certain items of interest.

That was emotional. Reading books my father owned, many on business theory or law, I was reading words that interested him, that were important to him. I felt like he was right there with me.

There are two books I recommend to most of the young people I work with. The first is "The Power of the Peddler" by Jeno F. Paulucci. Jeno was larger than life, one of those people who dominated a room just by walking in. Born into poverty on the Iron Range of northern Minnesota, Jeno suffered from ethnic discrimination but built empires in the food business, Chun King Chinese foods, Jeno's Pizza Rolls, and Michelina's Frozen Entrees.

I actually put a large property under contract with Jeno. I spent more than two years getting entitlements, the L&L Acres property. We were on the verge of closing when the Great Financial Crisis struck; Wall Street shut down, and lending came to a halt. We had to walk away. After the crisis faded, someone else picked it up and developed it into a beautiful community. Jeno passed in his early 90s.

I like this book because it's about never giving up, from humble beginnings to achieving a multibillion-dollar fortune. Jeno looked at every failure as a new beginning. He was amazing at thinking outside the box, and that's what young people need to understand. You have to think outside the box to be successful in anything, business or personal.

There will be things you can't control that feel like mistakes or aren't going the way you want. You need to do two things in this order: pray and pray often. Don't pray for money or things, pray for guidance, wisdom, strength, perseverance, passion. All the things that will put you in God's favor and help you accomplish what He's planned for you.

The second book is "Perseverance: Broke to Billions" by Chuck Whittall. Similar to Jeno's story, it starts in the early '80s, making it more relatable to younger people. It's a chronological blueprint of Chuck's adversities and successes that outlines the process of building a billion-dollar business.

Again, it's about thinking outside the box. I don't think schools today teach what kids need to go out and be successful. Sure, you can become an engineer or lawyer and get a job in those fields. But what about the kids who are entrepreneurs, who have what it takes to be successful in any field? They need that extra push to achieve great things.

1 Peter 5:2-3 says, "Be shepherds of God's flock that is under your care, watching over them, not because you must, but because you are willing, as God wants you to be... being

examples to the flock." That captures exactly how I feel about mentoring, being an example and watching over the next generation.

Many others have reached out asking me to sit with their young adults or friends. Most recently, a good friend on one of my boards asked me to meet with his daughter's boyfriend, just a sit-down to talk about vision and thinking outside the box. And you can bet I gave him those two book titles.

Another mentoring relationship that shows God's perfect timing is my friendship with Tyler Benzel. Tyler was a dedicated baseball player at Lake Highland Prep under the guidance of head coach Frank Viola. He'd travel an hour and a half each way to school to play for a better coach. That dedication paid off, he led the Highlanders to district and regional championships and earned all-state honors.

Tyler played college baseball at Louisiana-Lafayette before transferring to Florida Southern, where he graduated with a degree in Business Administration. After college, the Mets drafted him, and he played through their organization for a few years.

Tyler made it to spring training for the Mets, a huge accomplishment, the next step to the big leagues. But he got hurt in the first week or two, and his career went downhill from there. Like most baseball players whose careers end unexpectedly, he was asking, "What am I going to do now?"

Tyler had nothing to come back home to. That's when our paths crossed. I met him through his friend Ian, who came to work for us doing marketing. When I was looking for baseball coaches for Team Combat, I asked Tyler, "Want to be a baseball coach?" He said yes and brought tremendous knowledge to help young kids trying to get to the next level.

Tyler stayed with us through several years of travel ball. After we finished with travel ball, he attended Orangewood Christian School, where he was familiar with the coach. Tyler became one of my son James's coaches at Orangewood and was there all four years James played. He kept an eye out for him, helped him, and gave him extra insight and encouragement.

Tyler continued working with us through our business ventures. We provide third-party marketing services to brokerage firms worldwide. Tyler started doing training videos for their trading platforms. We wrote 200 videos, Tyler did voice-over work, and then we added images and graphics.

The funny thing is that Tyler didn't have any of those skills when we started. He'd read very monotone, with no voice inflection. If you've seen the movie "Up," you know the dog who says, "My master made me this collar so I could communicate with you", very flat and emotionless. We used to call Tyler "Doug" jokingly.

I worked with Tyler on improving his speaking skills, and he fully embraced the process. He did an amazing job of taking those training videos to the next level. We did this for third-party companies and PremiereTrade.

At that point, PremiereTrade had become stagnant and needed updated graphics and a new user interface. I said, "Okay, Tyler, you're ready. Let's do it." We created a complete GUI update. It was expensive, time-consuming work that required being methodical, but Tyler basically took on the entire challenge.

We'd brainstorm every day, and he'd carry out the vision. He managed teams of programmers worldwide, including those in Chicago, Ukraine, India, and other locations. We'd create documentation in PowerPoint, and Tyler would lay out the design, including tabs, flow, and functionality, all the way through to quality assurance and testing. He'd never had that background before, but he excelled at it.

It took two years to develop, and we rolled out the new version of PremiereTrade. When you talk about faith and God being in all the right places with a plan, Tyler is a perfect example. I needed Tyler as much as he needed me. He came to be a coach, became a great friend and great mentor to my son, and I helped him grow in many areas.

Then we started DX Developments, and Tyler was involved in our first three projects: Ciara Creek, University

Medical Center, and Halifax Plantation. Early days of Roan Bridge, Southern Pines, Crystal Ridge.

During this time, he met someone he'd gone to school with, a great woman a little older than him. They dated; I could tell this was the one. They got married at a local Catholic church during COVID with just immediate family, maybe 10 people. I was disappointed I couldn't attend, but I understood the restrictions.

Coming out of COVID, Tyler had to move on with his life. I was sad to see him go, but we parted as great friends and still are. We get together every couple of months for lunch. He worked for Chuck Whittall, who wrote that book I mentioned, and spent two years learning commercial real estate on billion-dollar projects.

Tyler had married the daughter of a prominent attorney and eventually went to work for his father-in-law, assisting with land development. But here's where God intervened in an amazing way, where He got involved in both our lives with a plan neither of us could have seen coming.

This attorney has a large technology business where they've created their own technology to manage leads from their practice, a massive operation with clients across the United States, requiring substantial technology needs. Tyler is now running the technology department, working with programmers to create back-office technology and user interfaces.

Tyler also developed and founded multiple mobile device applications, focusing on global market strategic investment portfolio diversification. As COO, he's responsible for key investments across multiple asset classes. Who would have known that all the work he did on PremiereTrade, learning to manage programmers worldwide, understanding user interface design, quality assurance testing, voice-over work, and business development, was all preparation for exactly where he is now?

He has a beautiful little daughter; everything is going great, and I'm so proud. It has been a blessing to have him in my life and see how God used our relationship to prepare him for his calling.

You know, speaking of people God puts in your life, I have to tell you about my business neighbor, John. Back in 2010, when PremiereTrade was winding down, I moved into my current office building. We still had a small server farm and a handful of employees, but things were slowing down. A couple of years later, we ended up downsizing to a smaller unit in the same building, just me and Rocky at that point.

That's when John moved his business into the larger office, I had previously occupied. Super cool guy, and we hit it off immediately. I remember he needed a garage door automated opener, and I gave him mine. He was amazed that someone he'd never met would do something like that for him, just a kind gesture because he was my new neighbor. John's a man of great Christian faith, his family were missionaries. They spent time in other countries preaching the Word, teaching, and helping locals. That faith foundation runs deep in him.

What I really admire about John, though, is how he runs his business with those same Christian values. It's not just a personal thing for him, he carries that faith right through his company and down to his employees. To be frank, I've always admired him for that. It's one thing to be a good Christian guy, which he is, but it's another thing entirely to build your business on those principles.

John has a son about the same age as my son, so they hit it off, too. However, what has been meaningful to me is that John has been here for more than ten years now. He ended up buying several units in the building and now owns the majority of it. I could have purchased my unit, and I always told him he could have it because he wanted to buy the whole building.

John's son, Jessie, whom I've known for more than 10 years, has turned out to be an amazing young man. He's now married, working, finishing school, and has aspirations to be a missionary, following in his family's footsteps. One time, they needed to borrow my forklift, and Jessie had never driven one. Instead of me doing the work for them, I told Jessie to jump up and do it. I taught him how to use it, and now he's an expert whenever they need it. The point is, I taught him the same way I would have taught my son.

John's daughter is a little younger and just finished high school. She was part of the Sheriff's Explorer program at the sheriff's office, where I was the president of the Sheriff Foundation. She has taken to that program.

However, I want to share something else about John: his faith has been a constant influence on me. We talk about God, about Christianity, about walking that walk every single day. And I mean every day, he's always asking how me and the family are doing, and I do the same for him. It's not just small talk. These are real conversations about life, about faith, about being better Christians.

John's been so impressed with my son James and his walk with Christ. He sees how James carries himself and how he talks about his faith, and John always encourages that. That means a lot to me as a father. When my son and his wife started their group at church, James was able to borrow the chairs from John that he needed each week, no questions asked, just something we do for one another.

We look out for each other too. If I'm here late and see something that needs attention at his place, I'll call him. If he notices something at my office, he does the same. It's one of those relationships where if you call, the other person shows up. That's community. That's what Christian brotherhood looks like in real life.

I think John's been an influence on me, specifically about constantly wanting to be a better Christian. Not in some big, dramatic way, but in the everyday stuff. How you treat people. How you run your business. How you show up for your neighbors. How you can speak boldly in a whisper about your faith.

That's what I mean when I say God puts people in your life at exactly the right time. John didn't just become a good business neighbor; he became someone who quietly challenges me to live my faith better every single day.

But perhaps the most significant mentoring opportunity God gave me came through baseball. My son played baseball, we started like most families with T-ball in Lake Mary in 2004-2005. His uncle RJ and I were coaching and had a blast. So did the kids. We taught real lessons about being on a team, winning and losing. I can tell you there were no participation trophies.

My son got pretty good at baseball. When he was 10, we were on a travel ball team heading to Cooperstown, New York. Last time, they had 10-year-old teams come up. But for me, it was on the plane ride up that God stepped in. We read in the paper that the travel ball organization's head coach had accepted a position coaching a college team in another state. I knew that meant no more travel ball with that organization. While in Cooperstown, I laid it all out, we started Team Combat.

But that wasn't the real story. The real story was bringing on former minor and professional baseball players to coach. I stayed on as a coach, too, and we were good. We traveled all over the country playing baseball.

But for me, it was about the kids. When the game was over, whether they won or lost, the coaches would meet in right field to discuss the game. I'd discuss what they learned on and off the field and how that would relate to their lives in the future.

One kid in particular, we'll call him Tommy, I immediately connected with. He was young and wore his emotions on his sleeve. He'd gone through a major traumatic event where a gruesome accident happened, and people were killed in front of him. You could see he was greatly affected. He and I built a bond, and for years, I worked with him on and off the field. It's amazing to see his growth over those years. I'm happy to say he's gone on to live an amazing life.

There were too many stories like that to tell, but all of them were gifts from God. He put these future leaders in front of me with this huge responsibility to say and do the right things. With God's help, I left it up to Him what to say.

Team Combat went on to have several teams and help lots of kids for nearly six years. At one point, I had 15 Division I players from my team's playing baseball. Today, I've two in the major leagues who used to play tournaments with us, at least four or five in the minors and countless others who have gone on to great careers and families. What a blessing this was from God.

There's more to thank God for. During this period, I was in transition with my business. The Great Financial Crisis was in full swing. I'd just come off the PremiereTrade run and was waiting for the economy to change.

Because of that, I was around more than ever with the family, more time with Deb, more lacrosse games with Jacki, and I attended nearly all my son's baseball games, more than 800 of them, and his practices. Something I'll cherish forever, and that's because God planned it that way. Sure, I worried about family and business, but in the end, I knew why it was so.

Speaking of PremiereTrade, I'd be remiss not to mention God's grace in that story. PremiereTrade was a significant part of my adult business life, and it's still in business after 20 years. One of my first employees, Rocky, is still with us running the technology side. We have over 3,000 users worldwide who use it daily to place trades. We built this technology from the ground up.

Rocky and I were talking about how God has a plan for us and PremiereTrade. Through all the adversity, the software is still in use, Rocky is still here running it, and people are signing up every day, more than at any time in the last 15 years. It's truly amazing, and I have my daughter

Jacki and her boyfriend working with me on the project. It'll be an amazing conclusion to that story sometime soon.

In baseball, you're always playing for your next coach. The lessons learned on the field are the same or similar lessons you'll learn in life. You're always performing in front of someone, your next employer, next friend, next pastor, who knows? However, you should be walking with God and growing your faith, even if you're starting. The journey never ends.

2 Corinthians 4:18 says, "So we fix our eyes not on what is seen, but on what is unseen since what is seen is temporary, but what is unseen is eternal." That's what I try to teach every young person I mentor, that the impact we make on others, the legacy we leave, the faith we pass on, these things are eternal.

I have to pause here and share something that just happened as I was writing this chapter. When I started Chapter 12, I had only 650 words and was struggling to complete it. It felt weak and inauthentic. I didn't know what to write or how to connect the themes, so I left it incomplete and went to church.

Still needing to finish it, I sat down an hour ago and started typing, but it was nothing. Then, like a bolt of lightning, it hit me, exactly what I needed to write. I proceeded to write 3,500 words, none of which was already written, only expanding on parts I'd barely mentioned elsewhere.

I say this because that is truly the power of God, guiding me in what to say. Even as I write this book, He continues to provide the words when I need them most.

Living the legacy means that every conversation, every time you mentor someone, and every example you set is building something that will last far beyond your life. You're investing in eternity through the people you touch and the faith you share.

That's what this chapter is really about - not just talking about faith but living it out. Faith that makes a real difference. Faith that leaves something behind. Faith that keeps going through the next generation.

# CHAPTER 13

# Humility And Grace

## *When Pride Meets Faith*

After Looking back, I think my struggle with pride and asking for help started when I was a teenager. In those years when I was struggling the most, especially financially, I would take odd jobs like mowing yards, washing cars, and whatever I could do to make some money. Maybe I was a little too young for a full-time job, but I was still motivated to be self-reliant. My mother was busy with her school, and my father wasn't really in my life except on rare occasions.

But on occasion, when I felt so overwhelmed and didn't know what else to do, I would have a conversation with my dad. It wasn't as easy as it sounds. He lived two hours away, and I wasn't able to just see him. He wasn't a phone conversation guy either, so usually, my experience of asking for help was face-to-face.

I was so overwhelmed with hearing "no" that it would nearly paralyze me with fear to even ask for something unless I knew the answer was going to be yes. It's a horrible feeling, and you're conscious of it even at a younger age. So essentially, what you do is don't ask. That same sentiment flows through this book.

But when I asked my dad for something, unfortunately, it was usually for money, he would say yes, he wanted to help. He always knew when I was really struggling; he could tell. But he would, on occasion, say, "We need to have a chat." To this day, it remains my least favorite saying.

This fear of asking for help is one of the reasons I experienced homelessness, even if just for a day or two. Even when you're older, you have to ask for help from those who love you and care for you, friends and family, when you need it. You have to let God work through them as well.

This experience fits well with what we're talking about in this chapter, pride meets faith. I certainly didn't realize it was my pride that was getting in the way, and my journey with Christ was still in its early stages. The faith was deep inside of me, waiting to come out.

As you've read to this point, it does come out, the experience of accepting Christ in Tampa at the youth convention, later taking a job cold-calling people. Can you imagine? Someone who gets anxious and is nearly paralyzed with fear of hearing "no" takes a job cold-calling and becomes a platform sales lecturer. That's faith. That's believing God's got something in mind for you.

After the collapse of PremiereTrade during the Great Financial Crisis, I found myself in a place I'd never been before, truly humbled. When you go from 250 employees to zero overnight, when a business you've built from the ground up disappears because of circumstances beyond your control, it strips away every ounce of pride you thought you had. I think that's when I realized something I'd never really understood before there's no place for pride when walking in faith. Maybe I needed to lose my business to learn that lesson.

I can remember starting a company called DNA Pulse after PremiereTrade fell apart. This time, I couldn't do it alone, I had to swallow my pride and make one of the hardest phone calls I'd ever made.

I called my Uncle Jack and his partner Nick and asked for help. These were successful men who were doing well, and here I was, someone who had once employed hundreds of people, who had built a multimillion-dollar company, having to ask for assistance. The old me might have been too proud to make that call. But losing the business had taught me something valuable: sometimes, our lowest moments prepare us for what comes next.

Proverbs 16:18 says, "Pride goes before destruction, a haughty spirit before a fall." I had experienced that fall, and now I was learning what comes after, humility that opens doors to grace and new opportunities.

Uncle Jack and Nick agreed to help, and together, we created a company that would essentially take institutional marketing online. I was working in marketing for a forex brokerage business, allowing them to convert leads into funded, active accounts. Through all of that, I learned a tremendous amount about marketing through social media platforms.

What happened was, every failure I'd experienced, every business challenge I'd overcome, every relationship I'd built, it all came together in this new venture. Scott Prewitt and I leveraged everything we had learned in the past. I discovered I could go into just about any business, have a conversation for 30 minutes to an hour, and come up with efficiencies to help take that business to another level. Even more so, I could help implement those suggestions.

James 4:6 reminds us, "God opposes the proud but shows favor to the humble." In my humbled state, I was learning what that really meant in ways I couldn't have imagined before.

It started with my stepmother, Jewel, and her husband, Steve. After telling them about the marketing work, I'd been doing, they gave me an opportunity to start doing marketing for one of their dealerships, a Chevy dealership. We leveraged the institutional knowledge we had gained from working with broker-dealers and developed marketing systems utilizing social media platforms to generate leads for car sales.

We would do Facebook advertising that generated leads, and then we created additional campaigns I called "I Got Mine." Any time somebody bought a car, we'd take a picture, post it on social media with "I Got Mine," and generate interest through that success story. The customers were as proud of the new purchase as we were of the sale. Steve and Jewel managed it like a family business.

But the real innovation was in the lead structure. We automated the entire system and created APIs that integrate our back-office systems with Facebook. Every GM dealer operates with DealerSocket; their lead management system is used nationwide. We created an API that integrated directly with DealerSocket.

As leads came in from Facebook, we automated the process so that when people clicked on our ads, they could indicate which car they were interested in, fill out a quick form without ever leaving Facebook, and the lead would be dropped directly into DealerSocket and then into the dealer's sales network. It was incredibly efficient.

From there, we expanded across other automobile dealership lines. My stepfamily also owns a Harley-Davidson dealership, so we applied the same system there. That was so successful that we ended up doing the same thing for about 15 other Harley-Davidson dealerships around the country, driving social media leads nationwide.

Scott and I, along with the team we put together, had decades of experience helping businesses grow. We created DNA Pulse, a sales and marketing company that recognized the heartbeat of a business as its customer acquisition pipeline. We leveraged our combined knowledge to automate the process, producing qualified leads and converting them into sales.

Here's what I learned: this success came because I had learned to humble myself and rely on my network of family and friends when I truly needed help. My willingness to set aside pride and ask for assistance created something that would serve not just me but many other businesses and their employees.

1 Corinthians 10:31 says, "So whether you eat or drink or whatever you do, do it all for the glory of God." That became my new approach to business, not building something just for my own glory but using the gifts I'd been given to serve others and create value that went beyond my success.

I remember being apprehensive when walking into businesses to offer advice. However, what I knew from my years of experience and faith was that I would be able to help the business owner. I needed to listen to the owner and their team, and then I could provide meaningful input and strategies that I could help implement.

I would always say a small prayer before one of those meetings, asking God to be with me and help me understand the business owner's needs, as well as provide valuable suggestions.

I learned to approach them with confidence, understanding that the principles I'd learned through the many different businesses I'd run over the years gave me the ability to look into situations and see where things might not be working or could work better. Sometimes, you can't see the forest for the trees, and maybe I had the perspective to help others see what they might be missing.

Before every meeting, I would pray for wisdom to have a good conversation and give valuable advice that could help others in their time of need. That prayer changed everything. Instead of walking in with arrogance about my abilities, I was walking in with dependence on wisdom working through me.

It was amazing how things changed. What started as a humble request for help evolved into a thriving business serving multiple industries. DNA Pulse grew into a well-performing company in just a few short years, all because I had learned to combine the practical knowledge from my past experiences with a humble heart that was open to direction.

Proverbs 27:2 says, "Let someone else praise you, and not your mouth; an outsider, and not your lips." I learned to let the results speak for themselves rather than promoting my abilities. When you approach business, or life, with humility and a genuine desire to serve others, doors have a way of opening that you never expected.

This period in my life taught me that our greatest failures can become the foundation for our greatest successes, but only when we're humble enough to learn from them and wise enough to seek help when needed. Pride tells us we have to do everything on our own. Faith tells us that we're meant to work through community, through relationships, and through our willingness to both give and receive help.

All that knowledge and experience led me to write a book called "The Ultimate Facebook Lead Machine," which captured everything we had learned about social media marketing and lead generation. The book was a way for me to memorialize what I learned, how I implemented it, and the successes and failures of each business. That's how I ended up with more than 11 books published.

I think seeing PremiereTrade falter during the Great Financial Crisis wasn't just a setback, it was preparation. Self-reliance was being stripped away so I could learn what real success looks like: using your gifts not just to build your empire but to serve others.

Every business conversation I had, every efficiency I helped implement, every lead system we created, it was all an opportunity to be a steward of the knowledge and experience I'd been given through both success and failure. When we approach our work with humility and a heart to serve, we discover that even our most challenging years can prepare us for a greater impact than we ever imagined possible.

The lesson of DNA Pulse isn't just about business success, it's about the grace that flows when pride gives way to faith, when self-reliance transforms into reliance on something bigger than ourselves, and when our greatest humbling becomes the foundation for our most meaningful contribution to others.

But as I wrote this, it dawned on me that I've done all of these books to remember my actions and experiences, to be able to recollect what I experienced and did. Until now, I had never realized that the most important lessons from those experiences, mistakes, and successes had not yet made it to the pages of one of my books, and that's exactly what I'm doing in this book on grace, my faith, and my Christian journey.

As I was writing this book and having conversations with people about the content and why I felt called to write it, I was reminded to make sure I wasn't being prideful. The Bible talks about that, and it's something I've thought about a lot. I've gone through this book several times to make sure I wasn't coming across that way.

My goal isn't to lift myself up or make myself look good. It's to talk about all my experiences, both good and bad, and how my spiritual journey has progressed to the point of writing this book. I want to share how I've recalled certain events that have lifted me to another level in my spiritual journey, and maybe that can help someone else who's struggling.

1 Peter 5:5-6 says, "Clothe yourselves with humility toward one another because God opposes the proud but shows favor to the humble. Humble yourselves, therefore, under God's mighty hand, that he may lift you up in due

time." That's exactly what I'm trying to do with this book, stay humble and let God use these stories however He sees fit.

So here it is. "Redeemed by Grace" is exactly what I needed to write. It rolls all my life experiences to date in chronological order, paying particular attention to the journey of faith and my walk with Christ. The first 16 chapters in this book are only the first installment of this journey, the most important book I have written and a roadmap to what comes next.

# CHAPTER 14

# It's Never Too Late

*God's Timing in Every Season*

You know what I hear from people as they get older? They feel like they're not prepared, or maybe they want to do more but don't know if they have time. "Am I prepared? Do I have enough time left to accomplish what I want?" And frankly, the whole idea of retirement just doesn't make sense to me for someone who still has dreams and goals.

I love addressing this perspective because it gets right to the heart of faith: remember, God has you where you need to be. You are right where He knew you would be. You just have to look around, open your eyes, open your heart to God, and let your experiences guide you to what you really should be doing and how you should be helping others around you.

If you're getting older in life, I think you should look at timeframes differently. Whether you're 70 (and 70 is the new 50), 80, or beyond, it doesn't matter. Gods still got something in mind for you. You just need to get up, take that step every morning, thank God for it, and carry out the plan of the day.

Psalm 90:12 says, "Teach us to number our days, that we may gain a heart of wisdom." This isn't about counting down to some end, it's about understanding that every day is a gift and an opportunity to serve God's purpose.

Here's something I tell people that completely changes how they think about their years ahead. Look at your life in increments, when you're younger, you can view those increments in 10-year periods, but over 60, use 5-year periods. Ask yourself: "What am I going to accomplish in that time frame?" Then, look back at what you've already accomplished in those increments.

I think about my journey and how this principle has played out. For me, I am still 3 years away from 60, so I will use the 5-year increment. In the last 5 years, I went through COVID, my son got married, I built DIX Developments from zero to over 15,000 units, I repositioned PremiereTrade, I had my 25th wedding anniversary, I founded two new sheriff foundations, I unlocked the next level of my faith, I have mentored some future leaders of America, met some amazing new friends, fostered some long-time relationships, and I am writing this book.

That's the last 5 years. I can only imagine what the next five years hold with all the new wisdom and experience I've gained. You can do the same thing.

But here's where it gets really exciting: this changes dramatically as you get older, with all that accumulated wisdom, experience, faith, and grace. The depth and impact of what I can contribute now, in my later years, far exceeds what I could offer in my younger years.

Isaiah 46:4 reminds us, "Even to your old age and gray hairs I am he, I am he who will sustain you. I have made you, and I will carry you; I will sustain you, and I will rescue you." God doesn't retire from His plans for us just because we age.

This verse should motivate you to understand: "Hey, there are a lot of things I'm going to get done and accomplish. I think God wants me to do all these things. I'm going to do all these things and help everybody I can."

I've had countless conversations with people who God has blessed to become very wealthy or successful, and they ask about retirement. Here's what I tell them: retirement doesn't necessarily need to be in the cards. If you've been given the blessing and ability to create wealth or make a significant impact, you need to take that gift and continue helping other people. Even if you feel you want to slow down, you can still serve others.

Continuing to serve ties back to what I mentioned earlier about creating foundations and engaging in philanthropic work. But it goes deeper than that. Your experience, your network, your wisdom, these are gifts that compound over time. The 65-year-old version of yourself has capabilities the 35-year-old version couldn't dream of.

I think about the mentoring I do now with young people. I couldn't have offered them the same value 20 years ago. I didn't have the failures to learn from, the relationships to leverage, or the spiritual maturity to guide them properly.

Maybe God was preparing me through every period, even the difficult ones, for greater service in later years.

Proverbs 20:29 says, "The glory of young men is their strength, gray hair the splendor of the old." There is honor and purpose in every stage of life, but something particularly powerful emerges with the wisdom that comes with age and experience.

I see this principle in action every day. The most effective board members I work with aren't the youngest, they're the ones who have been through multiple economic cycles, who have learned from their mistakes, and who have developed the judgment that only comes with time. They can see patterns, avoid pitfalls, and provide guidance that prevents others from having to learn everything the hard way.

Think about Paul, who wrote some of his most profound letters while imprisoned in his later years. Or Moses, who didn't even begin his major life's work until he was 80. Abraham was 75 when God called him to leave everything and follow His plan. Sarah was 90 when she gave birth to Isaac. God's timing doesn't follow human conventions about age and capability.

Romans 8:29 tells us, "For those God foreknew he also predestined to be conformed to the image of his Son." This transformation doesn't stop at a certain age, it continues throughout our entire lives. Every year brings new opportunities to become more like Christ, to serve more effectively, to impact more lives.

This transformation is why I'm so passionate about encouraging people not to see aging as a limitation but as preparation for their most significant contribution. Every relationship you've built, every skill you've developed, every lesson you've learned, both from success and failure, has all been preparing you for this period.

The foundations I've helped establish could only have been possible because of decades of business experience, relationship building, and an understanding of how to create a sustainable impact. The young people I mentor receive value from me now that I couldn't have provided 20 years ago. The business insights I can offer come from having built, lost, and rebuilt multiple companies.

When people ask me about retirement, I tell them to reframe the question. Instead of "When can I stop working?" ask, "How can I make my greatest contribution?" Instead of "How can I preserve what I've built?" ask, "How can I multiply the impact of what I've learned?"

Retirement should not mean you can't slow down or change pace. It means recognizing that your most valuable years might still be ahead of you. The compound effect of experience, relationships, and wisdom creates opportunities for impact that young people simply cannot access.

Every morning when I wake up, I thank God for another day and ask Him to show me what He's got planned for that day. Some days, it's a business meeting where decades of experience help solve a problem in minutes. Some days, it's a conversation with a young person where I can share insights that might save them years of struggle. Some days, it's work on the foundations that can only happen because of the network and resources God has allowed me to build over time.

The key is staying open to God's leading and recognizing that He's not done with you yet. Whether you're 50, 60, 70, or beyond, if you're still breathing, you still have purpose. The question isn't whether you have time left to make a difference. The question is whether you're willing to let God use the accumulation of your life's experiences for His glory and the benefit of others.

Don't let society's expectations about aging limit what God wants to do through you. Some of the most impactful people in history did their greatest work in their later years. They had to live through everything that came before to be prepared for what came after.

Your story isn't winding down; it's building to a crescendo. All those years of experience, relationship building, learning, failing, and growing were preparation for the impact you can make right now. God's been preparing you your whole life for this period. Don't waste it by thinking your best days are behind you.

They're not. If you're walking with God, your best days of service, impact, and contribution may very well still be ahead.

God doesn't waste a single period, and sometimes the best is truly saved for last. Let me share some stories that prove age is no limitation when experience and calling come together. Many of the most influential people didn't hit their stride until later in life.

Take Ray Kroc and McDonald's. Ray was 52 when he first met the McDonald brothers in 1954, but he didn't fully take over and expand the company until his early 60s. That's when he transformed McDonald's into a global franchise empire. He worked into his 80s, constantly pushing growth and innovation. Kroc once said, "The quality of a leader is reflected in the standards they set for themselves." You can see how years of life experience helped shape his discipline and vision.

He's a classic example of how preparation over decades can lead to massive success later, once the opportunity lines up with the right mindset and purpose.

Billy Graham started preaching young, but his most global influence came later in life. He preached to more than 215 million people in over 185 countries, with many of his largest crusades and television outreach efforts happening in his 60s and 70s. Even into his 80s, Graham's words continued to reach millions through broadcasts and writings. He often said, "God isn't finished with you when you turn 60 or 70, He may just be getting started."

Elisabeth Elliot became a well-known Christian author and speaker. Still, her most impactful ministry didn't begin until after her husband, missionary Jim Elliot, was killed by the Auca tribe in Ecuador. She was 29 at the time, but it was in her 40s, 50s, and beyond that her writing and speaking ministry took off. Books like "Through Gates of Splendor" and "Passion and Purity" influenced millions. Her depth came from her life experience, suffering, obedience, and endurance shaped her message and gave it weight.

Mary Kay Ash founded Mary Kay Cosmetics in 1963 at the age of 45 after being passed over for a promotion in favor of a man she had trained. She used $5,000 of her savings and launched a company based on biblical principles, including the Golden Rule. She built a business that empowered millions of women and became a household name. Her most fruitful years came after many setbacks, and God used her experience, not just her ambition.

Colonel Sanders didn't franchise Kentucky Fried Chicken until he was 65. After a long string of failures and jobs, everything from a steamboat pilot to a gas station operator, he used his first Social Security check to fund a trip pitching his chicken recipe to restaurants. Most turned him down, but his persistence paid off. By his late 70s, KFC had become a worldwide brand. His story shows that age is no barrier when God's timing is involved.

These lives prove that it's not about age, it's about readiness, faith, and obedience. If you've still got breath in your lungs, God still has a purpose in your path.

The list can go on and on. As you can see, age is not a hindrance. Gods got you where you need to be for a reason, and that's His timing, not yours.

# CHAPTER 15
# Always Becoming

## *The Journey Continues*

As I look back on everything I've shared in these chapters, one thing is certain, my walk with God is not finished. It's never been perfect. And it never will be. But it's mine. And I'm committed to growing in my faith for the rest of my life.

2 Corinthians 3:18 says, "And we all, who with unveiled faces contemplate the Lord's glory, are being transformed into his image with ever-increasing glory, which comes from the Lord, who is the Spirit." This transformation is ongoing, not a destination, but a journey of always becoming more like Christ.

Just recently, as I was wrapping up this book, I had lunch with Nick Nanton. As I was in the middle of writing about divine appointments and God's timing, I found myself asking as I walked into the restaurant, "I wonder what the reason is for Nick and I to be having lunch today?"

Yes, the obvious answer is to eat and catch up as we often do every few months, but this felt different. We were supposed to have lunch last month and had to reschedule, another small example of God's timing.

Nick started by telling me about a major business decision he made that we had discussed in our previous lunch. It was significant for him, something he had been doing for 15 years, and he felt it was time to move on. People often asked him, "Look where you are now; why are you still doing what you were doing?" Great question. Sometimes, as an entrepreneur, you become stuck in a business and don't know why or how to get out of it. It's not that easy. For Nick, it will take a few years to wrap up fulfillment obligations, but the decision to move on has set things in motion.

Nick is a man filled with faith. He, too, believes God has something in mind, and like me, he knows you are not in control of your plan. We talked about the fork in the road and how you know which way to go. That's simple, the way you go is the way that God planned you to go, so just embrace it.

I had two instances like that. The first was DNA Pulse, a successful business that we decided to end and finish fulfillment of the services we had already promised. For me, it was the end of something that was planned, that gave me purpose, paid the bills, and allowed me to move forward with God's will. But God had bigger things for me to do.

Jeremiah 18:6 reminds us, "Like clay in the hand of the potter, so are you in my hand." God is still shaping us, still molding us, still working on us through every business decision, every relationship, and every period of our lives.

The next example was DIX Generators, an authorized Generac dealer. This business started in 2019, just prior to COVID, and we created a successful business. Yes, again, that's God working in your life. You never know when the next step will come and what it will be. The more in tune you are with your faith, the closer you are to God, the easier it is to recognize that this is what God wants you to be doing today. And it can change tomorrow, not that it changes, it's just the continuation of God's plan.

The Generac business was a crazy run. In 2018, I added a whole-house generator to my home. Where I live, we experience numerous power outages throughout the year, and, of course, we are also affected by hurricanes. When I first installed my generator system, there were only about three in the community of 230-plus homes. So when the power went out, I had every light, every AC unit, and everything connected. It would look like an island of light in a sea of darkness, and I could stay that way for 10 days.

Fast forward to 2019. In my development business, there can be long periods of inactivity, especially when you have only one or two deals. So, to stay busy, we decided to become a Generac dealer. I remember that we were sitting around thinking about running an ad for a technician.

Talk about God's timing, I am sitting in my office, quiet, and I hear a knock on the door. I opened it to find a young man from Puerto Rico standing there, asking if I had any job openings for a generator technician.

Isaiah 65:24 says, "Before they call I will answer; while they are still speaking I will hear." God had answered my need before I even had a chance to place that ad. I couldn't believe this timing, or maybe I could, it was exactly what I was looking for at exactly the right time.

Axel lived in the apartments across the street. He had taken a chance and noticed there was a dealer across the street, so he thought he would just knock and see. I interviewed him on the spot. He was actually on his way to an interview with Caterpillar out by the Orlando airport. He called me the next day and accepted the job with us. One of the reasons was practical, he only had one car and lived across the street from us.

So, we got started. Axel was working for us as our technician. We had a truck equipped with a crane for him to drive, and he was able to go out and install generators on his own. That's kind of how we started. But if you look at all of those experiences that we've had over the past with all those other businesses, Scott Prewitt and I, who's been working with me for over 35 years in all these sales and marketing tech businesses, one of the biggest things we learned how to do was to automate those businesses. And so that's what we proceeded to do with the generator business.

We started running ads on Facebook, again, more experiences that we got from other businesses. We infused that into the generator business, and we started getting lots of leads for generators. We'd go out and run those leads, and what we found is that people have preconceived notions. Generac runs ads for whole-house generators for as little as $3,000, but typical generators are really more like $12,000 and up, depending on the type of house you have. So we'd drive an hour across town, have a meeting with someone, and they'd find out that it was going to be $12,000. So it was a waste of time.

We had a lot of leads, so we had to do something else. What I did was take those experiences, we knew algorithms back from our trading days, and we knew how to automate the leads. So we took the process, automated it, and turned it into what we called the "quick quote." Since then, we've actually done that in the AC business and other businesses as well.

Here's how we created the quick quote system. When someone clicked one of our ads on Facebook, we created a seamless transaction. They never left Facebook. They'd answer a few questions: How many ACs do they have? How many square feet? Do they live in a neighborhood with an HOA? And a few other things.

That lead would come through, and then we'd say, "Congratulations. Here is your estimate," and we knew it was already close to accurate. After that, we would ask them if they wanted to proceed, "Please take four photos following these examples." When we got the lead back with photos, we knew they were okay with the prices and that they had gone around the house and taken the four photos. That's when we'd call them.

We closed about 80% of those leads because the falloff happened before we ever got to a live conversation. We got so good at that process that we ended up selling generators without ever going to the customer's house until after the sale.

But the real story here isn't about marketing automation, it's about how God orchestrates circumstances for His purposes. When Axel came to see us, knocking on our door in what seemed like complete randomness, that's not a coincidence; that's God. Here was this Generac dealer across the street from where he lived, and we weren't even a store with retail traffic, we just installed, sold, and serviced generators.

The deeper story unfolded when we learned about Axel's situation. His daughter, who was 11 at the time, had leukemia. It was serious. She had to go through all of those treatments, chemo, hospital visits, the whole difficult journey that cancer families know all too well.

So, we made a commitment and said, "Listen, you'll never miss a day with your daughter, taking her to the hospital for her treatments." And that lasted for two years, being with her when she was sick when she'd lose her hair, through all the ups and downs. We paid him for all those times, provided him with a truck to drive, and adjusted our schedule to ensure he never missed any appointments. Additionally, we helped him with extra funds as needed.

Looking back, we realized something profound: the whole business had been orchestrated for Axel and his family. Think about it, where else could he have found a job with the flexibility for two years to be with his daughter, never missing a day with her, never missing a single treatment or appointment? We worked around all of that and still built a very successful business. It became too successful and took more time than we expected. Just as the development company started taking off and we needed to focus our attention elsewhere, we got the best news possible.

His daughter rang the bell. She was cancer-free.

It was like watching God's perfect timing unfold. Axel ended up moving back to Puerto Rico with his family, where he had more help and support from extended family members. We sold all the technology to another large electric company that wanted to start a generator division. They loved the quick quote system and were also in the air conditioning business, so we adapted the technology for their AC business as well.

1 John 3:2 tells us, "Dear friends, now we are children of God, and what we will be has not yet been made known. But we know that when Christ appears, we shall be like him, for we shall see him as he is." There's a mystery in our

becoming, but there's also certainty, we are being transformed into His likeness.

The point of sharing this story is to illustrate what I mean by "always becoming." You're walking God's path, and every day, something new is going to come up. The question is: will you embrace it? Maybe it's a new job, maybe a new business, new experiences for sure, but it's all part of the journey.

What looked like a random business opportunity became a vehicle for God to provide exactly what Axel's family needed during their most difficult periods. What seemed like a simple knock on the door was actually God's plan that would serve multiple purposes: giving us a business to run during a slow period, providing Axel with the perfect job situation for his daughter's treatment, and ultimately creating technology that would serve other businesses long after we moved on.

These random business opportunities are what the ongoing transformation looks like in real life. We don't always see God's purposes in the moment, but as we look back, the pattern becomes clear. Every relationship, every business venture, every challenge and opportunity, it's all part of becoming who God created us to be and serving His purposes in ways we might never fully understand.

I believe God has placed me in certain places at specific times for very specific reasons. Sometimes, I walk into a church service, and the message hits so deeply that I know it was meant for me. I didn't just happen to be there; I was supposed to be there. That same truth extends into every part of life, business, friendships, family, struggles, triumphs.

God does the same thing in my mentoring relationships, in board meetings, and in conversations with struggling business owners. I'll hear something in a sermon or read something in Scripture, and weeks later, I find myself sharing that exact insight with someone when God wanted them to hear it. Those aren't coincidences, they're God preparing me to be His instrument in someone else's life.

Romans 12:2 says, "Do not conform to the pattern of this world but be transformed by the renewing of your mind. Then you will be able to test and approve what God's will is, his good, pleasing, and perfect will." This renewal is ongoing, not a one-time event, but a daily choice to let God continue His work in us.

I've learned to embrace the process rather than rushing toward some imagined finish line. There is no finish line on this side of heaven. There's only the next step, the next opportunity to grow, the next chance to serve, the next moment to choose faith over fear.

When I mentor young people, I don't pretend to have all the answers or to have achieved some state of spiritual perfection. Instead, I share what I'm learning, what God is teaching me, and how I'm still growing. That authenticity often connects with them more than any polished presentation ever could.

So, if you're reading this and you're in a period of growth or maybe a period of questioning, I hope this reminds you that it's okay. Keep walking. Keep listening. Keep believing that you are exactly where God wants you to be, and that He's not done with you yet.

The story continues. The becoming never ends. And that's exactly as it should be.

# CHAPTER 16
# Still Writing My Story
## *A Living Testimony*

When I started writing this book just a week ago, the words flowed so quickly that I didn't have a chance to fully digest what I was putting on paper. The testimonial I want to share is that writing this book has been a revelation in itself. Since that first draft, I have read every Word, which has opened my mind and allowed me to remember things I haven't thought about in many years. That process allowed me to go back and add sections to the story, important lessons I have learned throughout my life that I had almost forgotten.

Many of the stories I have shared are ways to convey the Word of God and how it has shaped my life, the faith I feel and the grace I have received. The primary reason for writing this was that I know people struggle every day, and if just one person finds hope in this book, I have done my job. In addition, maybe some of my lessons or stories here give you that spark that you need to write your own story, start the next chapter, take your business to the next level, take more ownership of your job, and step up to be the leader God knows you are.

Writing this book helped me get my thoughts out that have been in my head for the last 15 years. I've written other books before, and I always receive feedback from people saying the words or strategies that the lessons helped them with. I think this one will, too.

My problem is that I am writing the last chapter of this book, but it won't be my last. Every day is a new chapter, new experiences, and a chance to spread the Word, boldly in a whisper. There are at least three stories in this book that were written this week. Imagine how many more in the next year, the next 5 years, those life increments I talked about earlier in the book.

Psalm 139:16 says, "Your eyes saw my unformed body; all the days ordained for me were written in your book before one of them came to be." Looking back, I can see that God was working in my life way before I even knew it. Every experience, setback, and breakthrough, I know that was all God.

What I've shared in this book is really just a collection of real stories and moments where God's timing was impeccable. I hope that in reading my story, you've found pieces of your own journey. Perhaps it brought back some forgotten memories or helped you think about things in a different light.

One thing I've come to realize is that we're never truly done with our story until God calls us home. Until then, we're all still writing it. I may be more settled in my faith now than I was before, but I still mess up. I still get it wrong. I still pray that I can be more consistent. But I think that's what God cares about: not that we're perfect, but that we keep trying.

A friend recently sent me a story that perfectly illustrates what I've been discussing with God's timing and perseverance. It's from Steve Harvey, and his story demonstrates exactly what I mean when I say our stories are never finished, and God's favor can change everything in a moment.

Steve Harvey was homeless, living in his car with only $35 to his name. He was ready to quit his dream of comedy and call his father to come home. But first, he decided to check his answering machine one last time. There was a message from Showtime at the Apollo, they wanted him to perform that Sunday night if he could get to New York. He was crushed because he didn't have the money to get there.

Then he discovered there was a second message that hadn't been there before. A comedy promoter in Jacksonville, Florida, had a gig that Friday night for $150. With $35 and three and a half hours to drive, Steve took the chance. He killed that night, and the club owner asked him to stay another night for another $150. Now he had $300.

He called Eastern Airlines; they had a $99 round-trip special from Jacksonville to New York. He parked his car at the airport and flew to New York with two bags. At the Apollo, he had to wait all day in a sixth-floor dressing room.

That night, he met D.L. Hughley, Dwayne "The Rock" Johnson, and Jamie Foxx, none of them famous yet all struggling comedians. One by one, they went on stage and got booed. Even Jamie Foxx, one of the most talented people in comedy, got booed off stage. Steve was terrified, but when his turn came, he had written a joke about Mike Tyson fighting Mitch Green in Harlem. The crowd went wild. He got a standing ovation and made $750 for one night, more than he'd ever made telling jokes.

That appearance led to hosting Amateur Night at the Apollo, then becoming the longest-running host in Showtime at the Apollo history, eight years. All because he didn't give up at his turn-back moment.

As Steve Harvey said, "In your life, everybody has a turn-back moment. You have a moment where you can go forward, or you can give up. But the thing you have to keep in mind before you give up is that if you give up, the guarantee is it will never happen. That's the guarantee of quitting, that it will never happen no way under the sun. The only way the possibility remains that it can happen is if you never give up no matter what because God is always coming. He's never too late."

Isaiah 43:19 reminds us, "See, I am doing a new thing! Now it springs up; do you not perceive it? I am making a way in the wilderness and streams in the wasteland." God is always doing new things in our lives, always opening new paths and always creating new opportunities for service and growth.

This perspective has changed how I approach every day. Instead of trying to control outcomes, I focus on being faithful in the moment. Instead of worrying about whether I'm doing enough, I concentrate on doing what's in front of me with excellence and integrity. Instead of being paralyzed by the magnitude of future possibilities, I take the next right step.

As I look toward what comes next, I know that more chapters are ahead. The sheriff's foundations will continue to grow and serve more families. The mentoring relationships will deepen and expand to touch more young lives. New business opportunities will arise that can serve God's purposes. My family will continue to grow in faith, and I'll have new opportunities to support and encourage them.

To those who've read along, thank you. If even one chapter spoke to your heart and stirred something in your spirit, then this was worth every minute spent writing it. I pray these words helped you see God more clearly in your own story.

More than that, I hope this book encouraged you to see your own life as a testimony worth sharing. You don't have to have achieved great business success, founded an art institution, or held a high-level position to have a story worth telling. You just have to have experienced God's faithfulness in your own unique circumstances.

Your testimony matters. Your journey has lessons that others need to hear. Your struggles have prepared you to help people facing similar challenges. Your victories can inspire others to keep going when they want to give up. Your faith, however imperfect, can encourage others to take their steps toward God.

Don't wait until you think you've got it all figured out to start sharing what God has done in your life. Start where you are, with what you have, with the story you're living right now. Someone needs to hear your testimony; maybe it's your story that will help change someone's life forever.

Remember Steve Harvey's lesson: you have a turn-back moment, but if you give up, the guarantee is it will never happen. The only way the possibility remains is if you never give up because God is always coming, and He's never too late.

Revelation 21:5 says, "He who was seated on the throne said, 'I am making everything new!'" Our God is in the business of new beginnings, second chances, fresh starts, and ongoing transformation. No matter where you are in your story, there are new chapters ahead.

Now it's your turn to experience the increments of your life, your next 5 years, 10 years, and create a lifetime of experiences, growing your relationship with God. The pen is still in His hand. The story is still being written. And the best may very well be yet to come.

Keep writing. Keep believing. Keep serving. Keep trusting.

The story continues. In you. Through you. Because of you.

# APPENDIX

## Bible Verses by Chapter

All Scripture quotations are taken from the New International Version (NIV) of the Bible unless otherwise noted.

### Preface

Proverbs 16:3 - "Commit to the Lord whatever you do, and he will establish your plans."

### Introduction

Proverbs 3:6 - "In all your ways submit to him, and he will make your paths straight."

### CHAPTER 1: The Early Years

Proverbs 22:6 - "Start children off on the way they should go, and even when they are old they will not turn from it."

1 Peter 5:10 - "And the God of all grace, who called you to his eternal glory in Christ, after you have

suffered a little while, will himself restore you and make you strong, firm and steadfast."

Isaiah 43:2 - "When you pass through the waters, I will be with you; and when you pass through the rivers, they will not sweep over you. When you walk through the fire, you will not be burned; the flames will not set you ablaze."

Ecclesiastes 3:1 - "To every thing there is a season, and a time to every purpose under the heaven."

## CHAPTER 2: Finding Jesus - *The Moment That Changed Everything*

Romans 10:9 - "If you declare with your mouth, 'Jesus is Lord,' and believe in your heart that God raised him from the dead, you will be saved."

2 Corinthians 5:17 - "Therefore, if anyone is in Christ, the new creation has come: The old has gone, the new is here!"

Jeremiah 29:11 - "For I know the plans I have for you,' declares the Lord, 'plans to prosper you and not to harm you, to give you hope and a future."

## CHAPTER 3: Wilderness Years - *When Faith Goes Underground*

Romans 8:28 - "And we know that in all things God works for the good of those who love him, who have been called according to his purpose."

Psalm 34:18 - "The Lord is close to the brokenhearted and saves those who are crushed in spirit."

1 Peter 5:7 - "Cast all your anxiety on him because he cares for you."

## CHAPTER 4: Standing On The Yellow Footprints - Finding Purpose Through Service

Psalm 103:8 - "The Lord is compassionate and gracious, slow to anger, abounding in love."

Jeremiah 29:13 - "You will seek me and find me when you seek me with all your heart."

Psalm 28:7 - "The Lord is my strength and my shield; my heart trusts in him, and he helps me."

Psalm 133:1 - "How good and pleasant it is when God's people live together in unity!"

Philippians 1:6 - "Being confident of this, that he who began a good work in you will carry it on to completion until the day of Christ Jesus."

## CHAPTER 5: New Beginnings - *Sobriety, Love, And Finding My Voice*

Proverbs 13:20 - "Walk with the wise and become wise, for a companion of fools suffers harm"

Ephesians 5:25-28 - "Husbands, love your wives, just as Christ loved the church and gave himself up for her... In this same way, husbands ought to love their wives as their own bodies. He who loves his wife loves himself."

Proverbs 27:17 - "As iron sharpens iron, so one person sharpens another"

1 Corinthians 2:4 - "My message and my preaching were not with wise and persuasive words, but with a demonstration of the Spirit's power."

# CHAPTER 6: Finding My Purpose -

*Writing, Speaking, And Giving Back*

1 Corinthians 1:27 - "But God chose the foolish things of the world to shame the wise; God chose the weak things of the world to shame the strong."

Philippians 4:13 - "I can do all this through him who gives me strength."

Colossians 3:23-24 - "Whatever you do, work at it with all your heart, as working for the Lord, not for human masters, since you know that you will receive an inheritance from the Lord as a reward. It is the Lord Christ you are serving."

Psalm 78:4 - "We will not hide them from their descendants; we will tell the next generation the praiseworthy deeds of the Lord, his power, and the wonders he has done."

# CHAPTER 7: Called To Serve - *ESGR And Learning To Trust God's Plan*

Isaiah 55:11 - "So is my word that goes out from my mouth: It will not return to me empty, but will accomplish what I desire and achieve the purpose for which I sent it."

Matthew 6:34 - "Therefore do not worry about tomorrow, for tomorrow will worry about itself. Each day has enough trouble of its own."

James 2:17 - "Faith by itself, if it does not have works, is dead."

Proverbs 3:5-6 - "Trust in the Lord with all your heart and lean not on your own understanding; in all your ways submit to him, and he will make your paths straight."

## CHAPTER 8: Fellowship, Testimony, And The Church - *Finding My Spiritual Home*

1 Peter 3:21 - "And this water symbolizes baptism that now saves you also---not the removal of dirt from the body but the pledge of a clear conscience toward God. It saves you by the resurrection of Jesus Christ."

Acts 2:41 – "Those who accepted his message were baptized, and about three thousand were added to their number that day. "

Acts 2:46-47 - "Every day they continued to meet together in the temple courts. They broke bread in their homes and ate together with glad and sincere hearts, praising God and enjoying the favor of all the people. And the Lord added to their number daily those who were being saved."

Hebrews 10:24-25 - "And let us consider how we may spur one another on toward love and good deeds, not giving up meeting together, as some are in the habit of doing, but encouraging one another---and all the more as you see the Day approaching."

## CHAPTER 9: Friends, Faith, And Intervention - *Divine Appointments In Relationships*

Galatians 6:2 - "Carry each other's burdens, and in this way you will fulfill the law of Christ."

Matthew 18:21-22 - "Then Peter came to Jesus and asked, 'Lord, how many times shall I forgive my brother or sister who sins against me? Up to seven times?' Jesus answered, 'I tell you, not seven times, but seventy-seven times.'"

Isaiah 55:8-9 - "For my thoughts are not your thoughts, neither are your ways my ways,' declares the Lord. 'As the heavens are higher than the earth, so are my ways higher than your ways and my thoughts than your thoughts.'"

1 Thessalonians 5:11 - "Therefore encourage one another and build each other up, just as in fact you are doing."

## CHAPTER 10: Faith-Based Entrepreneurship - *Building Businesses With God At The Center*

Proverbs 16:9 - "In their hearts humans plan their course, but the Lord establishes their steps."

Ecclesiastes 5:10 - "Whoever loves money never has enough; whoever loves wealth is never satisfied with their income. This too is meaningless."

James 1:2-4 - "Consider it pure joy, my brothers and sisters, whenever you face trials of many kinds, because you know that the testing of your faith produces perseverance. Let perseverance finish its work so that you may be mature and complete, not lacking anything."

Matthew 6:33 - "But seek first his kingdom and his righteousness, and all these things will be given to you as well."

Proverbs 21:5 - "The plans of the diligent lead to profits as surely as haste leads to poverty"

## CHAPTER 11: Called To Serve - *Time, Talent, And Treasure*

Matthew 25:40 - "The King will reply, 'Truly I tell you, whatever you did for one of the least of these brothers and sisters of mine, you did for me.'"

Acts 20:35 - "In everything I did, I showed you that by this kind of hard work we must help the weak, remembering the words the Lord Jesus himself said: 'It is more blessed to give than to receive.'"

2 Corinthians 9:7 - "Each of you should give what you have decided in your heart to give, not reluctantly or under compulsion, for God loves a cheerful giver."

Isaiah 6:8 says, "Then I heard the voice of the Lord saying, 'whom shall I send? And who will go for us?' And I said, "Here am I . Send me!" - "Each of you should give what you have decided in your heart to give, not reluctantly or under compulsion, for God loves a cheerful giver."

Galatians 6:9-10 - "Let us not become weary in doing good, for at the proper time we will reap a harvest if we do not give up. Therefore, as we have opportunity, let us do good to all people, especially to those who belong to the family of believers."

## CHAPTER 12: Living The Legacy -

*Mentoring The Next Generation*

Luke 12:11-12 - "When you are brought before synagogues, rulers and authorities, do not worry about how you will defend yourselves or what you will say, for the Holy Spirit will teach you at that time what you should say."

Philippians 1:27 - "Whatever happens, conduct yourselves in a manner worthy of the gospel of Christ."

2 Timothy 2:2 - "And the things you have heard me say in the presence of many witnesses entrust to reliable people who will also be qualified to teach others."

1 Peter 5:2-3 - "Be shepherds of God's flock that is under your care, watching over them---not because you must, but because you are willing, as God wants you to be... being examples to the flock."

2 Corinthians 4:18 - "So we fix our eyes not on what is seen, but on what is unseen, since what is seen is temporary, but what is unseen is eternal."

## CHAPTER 13: Humility And Grace -

*When Pride Meets Faith*

Proverbs 16:18 - "Pride goes before destruction, a haughty spirit before a fall."

James 4:6 - "God opposes the proud but shows favor to the humble."

1 Corinthians 10:31 - "So whether you eat or drink or whatever you do, do it all for the glory of God."

Proverbs 27:2 - "Let someone else praise you, and not your own mouth; an outsider, and not your own lips."

1 Peter 5:5-6 - "Clothe yourselves with humility toward one another, because God opposes the proud but shows favor to the humble. Humble yourselves,

therefore, under God's mighty hand, that he may lift you up in due time."

## CHAPTER 14: It's Never Too Late - *God's Timing In Every Season*

Psalm 90:12 - "Teach us to number our days, that we may gain a heart of wisdom."

Isaiah 46:4 - "Even to your old age and gray hairs I am he, I am he who will sustain you. I have made you and I will carry you; I will sustain you and I will rescue you."

Proverbs 20:29 - "The glory of young men is their strength, gray hair the splendor of the old."

Romans 8:29 - "For those God foreknew he also predestined to be conformed to the image of his Son."

# CHAPTER 15: Always Becoming - *The Journey Continues*

2 Corinthians 3:18 - "And we all, who with unveiled faces contemplate the Lord's glory, are being transformed into his image with ever-increasing glory, which comes from the Lord, who is the Spirit."

Jeremiah 18:6 - "Like clay in the hand of the potter, so are you in my hand."

1 John 3:2 - "Dear friends, now we are children of God, and what we will be has not yet been made known. But we know that when Christ appears, we shall be like him, for we shall see him as he is."

Romans 12:2 - "Do not conform to the pattern of this world, but be transformed by the renewing of your mind. Then you will be able to test and approve what God's will is---his good, pleasing and perfect will."

## CHAPTER 16: Still Writing My Story - *A Living Testimony*

Psalm 139:16 - "Your eyes saw my unformed body; all the days ordained for me were written in your book before one of them came to be."

Isaiah 43:19 - "See, I am doing a new thing! Now it springs up; do you not perceive it? I am making a way in the wilderness and streams in the wasteland."

Revelation 21:5 - "He who was seated on the throne said, 'I am making everything new!'"

## Summary

Total Bible Verses Used: 67 unique verses

Bible Version: New International Version (NIV)

Most Referenced Books: Proverbs (10 verses), Psalms (7 verses), Isaiah (7 verses), Romans (5 verses), 1 Peter (4 Versus), Matthew (3 verses), Jeremiah (3 verses)

www.ingramcontent.com/pod-product-compliance
Lightning Source LLC
LaVergne TN
LVHW041213080426
835508LV00011B/932